# Dimitri's Cross

## The Life & Letters of St. Dimitri Klepinin, Martyred during the Holocaust

*Hélène Arjakovsky-Klepinine*

*Translated from the French by the monks
of the Monastery of St. John of San Francisco*

CONCILIAR PRESS MINISTRIES ☩ BEN LOMOND, CALIFORNIA

Dimitri's Cross:
The Life & Letters of St. Dimitri Klepinin, Martyred during the Holocaust

Original French text copyright © 2005 Hélène Arjakovsky-Klepinine
English translation copyright © 2008 Conciliar Press Ministries

Published by        Conciliar Press Ministries
                    P.O. Box 76
                    Ben Lomond, CA 95005-0076

Originally published in France as *Et la vie sera amour*
by Les Éditions du Cerf–sel de la terre, 2005

All Old Testament quotations, unless otherwise identified, are from
*The Orthodox Study Bible,* © 2008 by St. Athanasius Academy of Orthodox
Theology (published by Thomas Nelson, Inc., Nashville, Tennessee) and
are used by permission. New Testament quotations are from the New King
James Version of the Bible, © 1982 by Thomas Nelson, Inc., and are used by
permission.

Printed in the United States of America

ISBN 10: 1-888212-33-0
ISBN 13: 978-1-888212-33-4

Cover and interior designed by Katherine Hyde

Cover background photo: Fence at Auschwitz (shutterstock.com)

# Contents ∞

# Preface ∞

∞ *I*T IS NOT EASY TO BE THE DAUGHTER OF A PRIEST AND A saint. It is so difficult to write his biography without turning it into either a eulogy or a hagiography that I started five times over before daring to really begin. It was my children who pushed me to do it. They wanted to know this grandfather they never met, yet about whom everyone speaks. I told them I didn't know him either, or just barely . . .

I was only five when the Gestapo came to arrest my father in February of 1943 and barely six when he died on February 9, 1944, in a concentration camp at Dora, near Buchenwald. All the same, I can dare to say that I've lived my whole life with him. For me as a little girl, my papa and priest—whom I never saw dressed in anything other than a cassock or vestments—had simply gone to his "Master." Having celebrated his last liturgy, he closed the curtain of the royal doors[1] and went on to "where the saints repose."[2] It was rather obvious that I wasn't sad about his death. What weighed me down were my mother's tears, her loneliness and helplessness. By a sort of grace, this absent father of mine nevertheless remained present my whole life; I felt that he was with me. This certainty is hard to express in ordinary words.

This biography will inevitably be both imaginary and hagiographical, and I claim its intuitive and emotional character as my right. It will be based on the many documents I have at my disposal: memoirs

1 Doors in the center of the iconostasis which, in Orthodox churches, unite the sanctuary and nave.
2 Text taken from the Orthodox funeral service.

written by my mother, aunts, and grandfather, as well as a number of testimonies written by parishioners. Forever faithful to the memory of their pastor, this group would gather for a memorial service on each anniversary of his death, after which some would speak, sharing their memories. They were generally published in a parish bulletin or the RSCM's[3] Messenger, issues meticulously collected by my mother, who treasured everything.

A decisive event took place in 1985. On the occasion of the fortieth anniversary of the death of Mother Maria Skobtsova, the RSCM organized a large commemoration gathering attended by her authorized biographer Fr. Sergei Hackel, her friend Elisabeth Behr-Sigel,[4] as well as her co-prisoners at Ravensbrück, Rosane Lascroux and Geneviève de Gaulle.[5] I was also invited to recall this remarkable Orthodox nun who saved the homeless and Jews from persecution under the Occupation and who died as a martyr. Since my father had been the rector of the parish Mother Maria established at 77 Lourmel Street[6] and shared in her action of resistance as a martyr, he was mentioned by the chairman of the commemoration, Michael Sollogub.

A while later, Fr. Nikolai Ozolin invited me to record a television program on Mother Maria. While we were recording, the program's editor, Maxime Egger, asked my friend Françoise Lhoest and me to gather and translate a certain number of the saint's writings.[7] One thing led to another, and I also became Mother Maria's biographer. Ten years later, encouraged by Orthodox friends, I compiled a document in support of her canonization, intended to be sent to Bartholomew I, Ecumenical Patriarch of Constantinople. Thus I was led to compile resources and to discover certain new facts concerning my father, Dimitri Klepinin.

3  The Orthodox youth movement "Russian Student Christian Movement" (RSCM; in French l'Action chrétienne des étudiants russes [ACER]) was established in 1923 by Russian émigrés with its headquarters in Paris. Its history will be referenced later on and it will be referred to as the Russian Student Christian Movement or RSCM.

4  Elisabeth Behr-Sigel (1907–2005) was an Orthodox theologian, author of many works on Eastern Orthodox spirituality and the role of women in the Church.

5  Geneviève de Gaulle-Anthonioz (1920–2002), niece of General Charles de Gaulle, entered the Resistance at the age of twenty and was confined to Ravensbrück. After she returned alive, she dedicated her life to the destitute through the association ATD Fourth World, of which she was president.

6  This house no longer exists. A plaque was affixed on the building at this number in February of 2003. This location will later be referred to simply as Lourmel.

7  Le Sacrement du Frère, Pully et Paris, Éditions du Cerf-sel de la terre, 1995 and 2001.

Some of my friends said to me, "You did this work for Mother Maria, why not do the same for your father?" Alas, it's been much more difficult to write about a quasi-mythical father and to separate what I know of him from what I've imagined. This seemed so arduous that I revised it at least a hundred times. This went on until favorable circumstances arose and a number of supportive friends no longer let me use this difficulty as an excuse, persuading me that a daughter can write her own father's biography. It is a text that will not have the rigor of a canonization document or a historical treatise, but will allow intuition and dream to play a part.

# ❧ I ❧

# *Prologue*

# Dora, the Man-Eater ∞

∞ *F*R. DIMITRI KLEPININ, ORTHODOX PRIEST, PRISONER NUM-
ber 38,890, died at Dora in Germany in the middle of the night of February 9, 1944. One year earlier to the day, after celebrating his last liturgy as a free man, he surrendered to the Gestapo at Saussaies Street
in Paris.

I'd long imagined a pilgrimage to Dora but feared the emotion,
pain, and horror of such a visit. Finally, I was persuaded to go after
hearing about a trip in the spring of 2001 organized by people who had
once been prisoners in the camp. They planned to meet several times
with some German youth from Thuringe and Lower Saxony, who were
going to participate in a rather innovative and hopeful event called
"the Life March."[1]

We set off with a group of veterans who had been imprisoned at
Dora at the age of 20. They planned to recount what they suffered between 1943 and 1945 to a group of German high school students. These
veterans were all between seventy and eighty years old. I greatly respect
their youthful spirit and vigor, something particularly moving when

---

[1] After studying with their teachers the reality of the Holocaust in their region dotted with camps, these young people read the pilgrimage participants' biographies
and dedicated three days to listening to their experiences. They then retraced the
murderous Death March taken by those who still survived in 1945 when the death
camps were torn down. They placed monuments which they made during the ac-
ademic year at the execution site. This initiative came from the son of a deportee,
Jean-Paul Thiercelin, and from an energetic French teacher at Gottingen, Renée
Grihon.

you know what they suffered during their internment. Most had been arrested for acts of resistance. Certain others were generals who had known Charles de Gaulle and Edmond Michelet.[2] They admitted that for a long time they had hated the Germans, but little by little they began to forgive them.[3] For me also, the march had the purpose of encouraging forgiveness, as well as that of helping me understand exactly what my father endured in this hellish concentration camp.

The veterans presented a brief history of Dora. The internment and complete exploitation of the enemy constituted an integral part of the doctrine of the Nazi totalitarian system. From the time he took power on January 30, 1933, Hitler opened concentration camps where he sent the Germans who opposed him. These camps included Dachau in Bavaria and Oranienburg near Berlin. The system had the two goals of suppressing and liquidating the adversary and of exploiting free manual labor, since manual labor was something generally looked down upon.

Buchenwald, near Weimar, opened in 1938. Most of the other camps, collectively known as Kommando, were built beginning in 1942 in hundreds of locations as supplementary detention sites. Dora began as a Buchenwald annex and later became a self-sufficient camp in October 1944. Unlike Auschwitz, Dora was not intended as a place of extermination or immediate death. Rather, everything there was organized so as to reduce the prisoner's life expectancy to no more than three weeks. This was especially true during the period between September 1943 and May 1944. Later on, when Dora's underground factory began to produce V2 rockets, the conditions of life improved and the death rate declined slightly.

Prisoners at the camp included people from as many as thirty different countries. Russians and Ukrainians made up the majority. Considered subhuman by the Nazis, they received less food than others. Of

2  Beginning in 1940, Edmond Michelet, a Catholic member of the Democratic-Christian Movement, put a resistance network in place and helped numerous victims of the Vichy regime. Arrested in 1942 and deported to Dachau, he became a providential support for a number of his co-prisoners. He served as a minister during the Fifth Republic.

3  In 1997, the admirable Jean Mialet, a French officer born in 1920 who was arrested in 1943 for acts of resistance and then deported to Buchenwald and Dora, published the book, *Hatred and Forgiveness*. The point in question was not to forget, but to forgive and do whatever possible so that it would never happen again.

the more than 60,000 prisoners who came through Dora, 20,000 died. In February 1944, when Fr. Dimitri passed away, the number of dead was so great that it became a real nightmare to transport their corpses to Buchenwald's crematorium. The following month, the administration decided to build a crematorium at Dora itself. (Dora was both a woman's first name and the code name for the Mittelbau I construction site, which would thenceforth be known as "The Man-eater" by its inmates.)

At the end of 1943, Fr. Dimitri's close friend George Kazachkin arrived at Dora after being arrested the previous February for his involvement with the social aid group Orthodox Action.[4] Upon his arrival at the camp, nothing except some gypsum quarries existed yet on that Harz mountain called Kohnstein. The work of the new arrivals involved setting up the camp and its underground factory. Transported from Buchenwald in enclosed trucks and trailers, the workers faced a constant threat of beatings and were forced to travel squatting in order to keep from falling over. At Dora, they dug a tunnel and with difficulty, forced a passage through gravel, wood planks, and masses of fallen earth, all in a cold, humid, and gloomy atmosphere. The darkness, mugginess, and mine explosions only added to the hellish atmosphere, brought to completion by the yelling SS officers and savage cries from the *Kapos* (prisoner guards armed with batons).

George Kazachkin had studied at the School of Bridges and Highways, a prestigious civil engineering school in Paris. This is what ultimately saved his life. He was assigned to the architects' section of Dora, a job that involved construction of wooden barracks on the tunnel's exterior as well as access roads to the railway 50 kilometers away that connected Dora to Buchenwald. George had the privilege of working as a draughtsman in an administrative building. Thus he was able to traverse the immense grounds of the growing camp. However, Dora had no sooner been built than corpses were being sent to Buchenwald by the hundreds, which made this annex into a living hell.

On January 15, 1944, George learned that Fr. Dimitri would be in the last transport coming from Buchenwald to Dora. He barely recognized

---

4 Orthodox Action was an organization whose aim was to consolidate the charitable and social efforts of Russian émigrés in France. It was founded by the Russian Orthodox nun Mother Maria Skobtsova on September 29, 1935. In blessing the association, Metropolitan Eulogius declared, "Dedicate yourselves to the lowliest."

his old friend in that emaciated prisoner with a wrinkled face and a shaved head, wearing striped clothing marked by a red political triangle stamped with an "R" for Russian. "Why Russian?" he wondered. Fr. Dimitri had been one of the 38,000 French people transferred from Compiègne in December of 1943 and should have worn an "F". George later learned that during the quarantine in Buchenwald, the priest had chosen to register as "Russian" in protest against the treatment of prisoners from the USSR. In addition to this, he was given excavation work since his records mentioned that he was a priest.

For a long time I believed that my father had escaped the worst, this tunnel about which I had read some atrocious descriptions. With one voice, the Dora veterans informed me that it meant certain death to be sent to "excavation work"—as they called it—during the winter of 1943–1944. In this immense sediment-covered construction site, the prisoners were forced to carry sheets of plasterboard so heavy that four men could barely carry one, while another group of prisoners took cartloads of rubble out of the tunnel, certain that they would receive blows from the baton at even the slightest mistake. The camp's hilly and muddy grounds were such that one could imagine the amount of effort the undernourished men had to exert in order to hoist blocks and boards to the top of the hill. Ongoing cries accompanied this scene in the cold of dawn.

Upon entering the camp today, one can't help but be struck by the *Appelplatz,* an immense square capable of holding up to 14,000 men in close ranks. In January of 1944 the square was a field of frozen beets. Roots would still grow up here and there, which the prisoners gathered and quietly sucked. Today, the camp's buildings have all been reconstructed, the bunkers and the gallows, along with a train car on twelve meters of rail. It was at these sinister gallows that new arrivals were gathered and forced to watch the swinging, gaping-mouthed bodies of its victims.

There were few SS soldiers at the camp, and a number of prisoners took up the role of maintaining discipline as a means of avoiding starvation. These included *Stubendienst* (responsible for the barracks), *Schreiber* (responsible for keeping a headcount), *Vorarbeiter* (work foremen), and *Kapos* (who were armed with batons). This survival strategy ended pathetically as most of these people were lynched in 1945 by the surviving prisoners.

Two barracks have been rebuilt on the wooded slope. I asked where I could find the *Schonung* or office of work exemption where Fr. Dimitri died. The veterans answered in chorus, "Up there." On Sunday, April 22, 2001, the place where the office once stood is now a butte planted with beech trees and dotted with violets. Everything is calm. I sing in a low voice, "Give rest to the souls of Thy servants." A few steps from the crematorium, where a memorial has been built, I feel as if I'm in an open-air church.

In February 1944 there was still no crematorium. My father's body must have been thrown out the window and taken by armored car with others who died that night to a train headed for Buchenwald's crematoriums. I scraped the ground and picked a few blue flowers coated with clay when a thought came to me—what killed Fr. Dimitri was having to witness such an intense concentration of hatred beating down on human beings reduced to the condition of slavery, with a single goal—to save their skin. The only thing he could still do was to die for and with them, "on behalf of all and for all." Jean Mialet confirmed this for me. Almost all the priests in this camp perished. Amidst this hell, they tried everything and dared all to practice their priesthood by hiding the Eucharist on their persons, hearing confession in the latrines, giving absolution to the dying, all while facing harassment from the Kapos.

The anthology *Memorial of the Dora-Ellrich Camps* recognized the priests' admirable work at Dora:

Not a single convict priest will fail to intensely reinvigorate his priesthood and better understand his role as a man who must be all things to all men [1 Cor. 9:22]. [. . .] No pen could write his secrets, his conversations or his consolations. This gladsome light was witnessed one night by Charles:

"I've watched you for four Sundays. I don't know what you could say or give to those who come to you, they arrive completely sullen but leave with transfigured faces.

—Most know that I carry the Good Lord [the Eucharist] on me and many confess and take communion.

—Now there, old chap, is some bravery."

Dora would come to confirm the phrase: "The blood of the martyrs is the seed of the Church."

The Abbot Bourgeois: Dead

Fr. Dimitri Klepinin: Dead

The Abbot Jean Courcel: Dead

The Seminarian Jean Ficheux: Dead

The Heavenly Father took them in the midst of their work, even as they voluntarily offered up their lives for their suffering brothers.[5]

The Nazis understood that "clerics, bishops and other *Bibelforscher*" had the power to delay the degradation of their victims by raising morale. Helping one's neighbor, then, was a crime. The Nazis delighted in trying to deride this power. At Christmas, a large decorated fir tree was placed at the camp's entrance. That night, a Hungarian orchestra was summoned to play joyful gypsy tunes as those who did not cooperate were simultaneously being hanged. These terrible blasphemies against the Holy Spirit must have hurt the priests even more cruelly than the lice, beatings, hunger, and cold. Fr. Dimitri had seen this Christmas tree at Buchenwald, then, ten days after coming through the camp's gate. Upon it was inscribed "To each his duty." It was then that he understood that his "duty" as an Orthodox priest would be to bear his cross to the very end.

After fifteen days at Dora, Fr. Dimitri resembled an old man, a "Muslim" as they would say in camp jargon. Couldn't they do something for that old man? George and his friends resolved to do something to allow him to be exempted from excavation work. They approached a Russian Kapo, who agreed to intervene with the foreman on his behalf. The foreman called him up, *Häftling* (inmate) 38,890, and asked his age. "I'm 39 years old," Fr. Dimitri responded. Thinking he was being mocked, the foreman hit the priest with his club, and Fr. Dimitri remained in excavation.

"Will you hang in there?" his worried friends asked him.

"Yes," he replied with a weak smile, "but not for long."

Fr. Dimitri contracted pleurisy, but because the infirmary was full, he was sent to the exemption bureau, which had been transformed into a death house. There, sick people slept on the ground amidst excrement and a suffocating odor. George Kazachkin succeeded in finding Fr. Dimitri, though he was very weak. George was present at a visit

5 *Memorial des camps de Dora-Ellrich*, Paris 1949, pp. 42–43

by a German doctor, who upon learning that Fr. Dimitri was a priest, declared in a sententious tone, "Keep your spirits up. A priest has to be a courageous example for his comrades." This remark did nothing but rub salt on Fr. Dimitri's wounds. He was going to die, and he admitted to George that he felt abandoned by God.

The next day, for the first time ever at Dora, stationery was distributed to the prisoners so they could write to their families. George brought a letter to the Schonung for Fr. Dimitri. The priest, however, had already lost the ability to speak and gestured to him that he wouldn't be able to write. The curfew bell sounded, and before hurrying back to his barracks, George promised Fr. Dimitri he would come back the next day to help him write to his family in Paris. When he came back the next day, on February 9, Fr. Dimitri's body had already been piled up with the others who had died during the night.

Until recently, George's description served as the sole account of my father's suffering—that of an emaciated man in striped pajamas, with a shaved head, spread out on dirty straw and holding a blank card with a stamp bearing the image of Hitler: a card we never received.

Providentially, in 1995, I received an additional testimony. A Russian prisoner working in the tunnel had witnessed Fr. Dimitri's death. Knowing he would die in the tunnel, the prisoner had accepted the position as a Kapo. What was he doing at the Schonung that night? We will never know for sure. However, he recognized the priest as someone for whom his friends had asked him to intervene, and overcome with pity, he bent over him. Recognizing a compassionate face, Fr. Dimitri asked the Russian to make the sign of the cross with his lifeless hand. Taken aback, the prisoner signed the priest, who then breathed his last.

Fr. Dimitri's death triggered something powerful in this man's heart. After he was liberated, he went to the monastery of the Protection of the Mother of God, in Bussy-en-Othe (Burgundy, France). He made a rather somber impression on the nuns there, as of one deeply troubled. So they prayed for him. One day he threw a fit and reduced the sister responsible for cleaning his cell to tears. Ashamed, he began to confess to her. He was tormented by the idea that he would forever have to live with the way he had treated his fellow prisoners at Dora. He told her how he had found himself faced with the death of a "just man." That image of the sign of the cross haunted him—he whose hand was soiled by the countless blows he had laid on the backs of his fellow prisoners.

"What was this priest's name?" asked the nun, Mother Maria Iglitskaya.

"Fr. Dimitri Klepinin."

When the nun narrated this exchange to me, she added, "Since that day, I've prayed to your father as a saint." This moved me a great deal.

I was all the more affected by this unexpected witness when I called to mind an episode from my father's infancy, related to me by his aunt, Anna Hippius. The Russian Kapo's movement of making the sign of the cross with the dying priest's inert hand echoed an instance from Fr. Dimitri's childhood. His family had gathered at the crib of an infant only a few months old. The baby's mother lifted its hand to bless the family with the sign of the cross. That baby was Fr. Dimitri.

# II

# *Childhood in Russia*

# The City of the Five Mountains ✂

✂ IN ORDER TO RECALL DIMITRI KLEPININ'S CHILDHOOD, I feel that I need to speak to him directly, and having survived him for sixty years, to address the child he was. For his parents, he was a fragile child who was destined for a brilliant life that was so complex and at the same time so endearing that I feel the desire to take up his mother's perspective. Thus I transition from daughter to mother. I hope the reader will pardon me for this incongruity.

So, Dima,[1] I'll address you directly. You are no longer my parent, but once again a little child.

I went to the city where you were born, in the northernmost region of the Caucasus. I breathed in the air and found our family's tombs at the cemetery. They showed me the church your father built. I have a picture of the house where you were born. A few years later, I saw Odessa, where you spent your childhood and from which you were driven by the Revolution. The municipal archives there contain traces of the Klepinin family, including the houses your father built and the library your mother co-founded. I saw the church you entered and from which you were chased by a merciless nun on one infamously anguished day.

Before visiting, I didn't know much about this Pyatigorsk, the city of the five mountains in the first foothills of the Caucasus. I only knew that it was the city where you were born. Only that and nothing else—a

1   Diminutive for Dmitri.

birthplace and a point on the globe, almost an abstraction. Is it really important to be born in a certain place?

Mother was born in the north near St. Petersburg, thousands of kilometers from the five mountains. Nothing would have brought you and your wife together if it weren't for the October Revolution, emigration, and involvement in the Orthodox youth movement established in Paris. It was France that brought you together, or rather, the Russian Diaspora, that little Russian island surrounded by a rough French sea which was if not hostile, then at least indifferent.

The day I saw the Caucasus, I felt that the place where one is born is not insignificant. Every living child receives a certain mark from his birthplace. It forms his personality and models his behavior, and then perhaps it is passed on to his children. In the collective Russian memory, Pyatigorsk is associated with the great romantic poet Lermontov.[2] It was there that he came as a child on vacation with his grandmother and where he was later exiled. There he composed one of his most famous poems, "I come out alone onto the road," and there he died in a duel in 1841 at the age of 27. I wonder, what did Lermontov mean for you, Dima? Was he your poet? Did the music of his lyrics move you? If I really liked Lermontov before even knowing that he lived in the city of your birth, is it because of some mysterious transmission from you?

Pyatigorsk is a city of water, of spa-goers. It makes up part of a complex of watering places renovated under the impulse of Doctor Mikhail Zernov[3] at the beginning of the twentieth century. It was Dr. Zernov who organized a large construction plan for this site.

This is where the Klepinin family entered the scene. Both your father, Andrey Nikolayevich, a civil engineer and architect, and your mother were originally from the Urals. They had owned an estate near Yekaterinburg at Nikolskoye. At the end of the nineteenth century, wealthy Russians who were used to bathing at Baden-Baden or in "Roulettenburgs"[4] discovered the virtues of their own national mineral water. A

2  Mikhail Lermontov (1814–1841) remarkably expressed the nostalgia of those who, a short time before, had listened to the celestial songs and could no longer bear the disharmony of earthly sounds.

3  A medical doctor and specialist in thermal treatments, Mikhail Zernov (1857–1938) contributed to the rise of the Caucasus watering towns. The Zernov children were very close to the Klepinins.

4  This alludes to the fact that the watering towns also had a casino where clients could "play their luck," as Fyodor Dostoyevsky described in his novel, *The Gambler.*

vast bathing complex was built in the northern Caucasus, and Andrey Klepinin was invited to work on a large site a few kilometers from Pyatigorsk. They entrusted him with constructing the bathhouse at Kislovodsk, an immense and elegant edifice inspired by the Rajasthan palaces. So he moved his family to Pyatigorsk. It was here that his children would be born: Nikolai in 1899, Tatiana three years later, and finally you on April 14, 1904.

You were baptized as Dmitri in memory of St. Demetrios the Myrrhgusher,[5] a young military officer from Thessaloniki who refused to renounce his faith and consequently died as a martyr. The writer and philosopher Dmitri Merezhkovsky was your godfather. Zinaida Hippius, his wife and your mother's cousin, was a woman of letters with a caustic way of writing.

Having just escaped pneumonia after birth, you were quite small and fragile. Anna, one of the Hippius sisters who dearly loved you, recalled this significant episode. The house was plunged in distress as the doctors predicted your end. Your mother Sophia invited your two grandmothers, your father, and your aunts to come to your room, where, pale, you were breathing in an oxygen tent with great difficulty. The hour had come to say farewell to you. Everyone approached with a heavy heart. Your mother, in a sudden surge of inspiration, took your little hand and, joining its fingers, blessed those who were in the room. Thus, as a dying infant, you blessed the congregation. It was an unusual and touching moment that made everyone leave feeling moved. The crisis passed that night, and you were saved.

Anna would recall this movement and your little hand when, thirty years later, as you were being ordained a priest, you came out from the sanctuary for the first time to bless the faithful. At that solemn moment of the liturgy, which parishioners always await with fervor, that first blessing from a dying child seemed like a mysterious foreshadowing of the later pastoral blessing.

Your mother Sophia Klepinina's gesture was not so surprising. She was profoundly religious, one might even say mystical. In her personal journals, which I possess, she composed prayers, unceasingly

5  Named general of the army of Thessaloniki and proconsul of Greece, St. Demetrios lived in Thessaloniki, of which he is the patron saint today. He was martyred under the reign of the emperors Diocletian and Maximian (284–305) and is commemorated by the Orthodox Church on October 26.

dialoguing with God. Moreover, she was a well-informed teacher who, unhappy with the level of the educational institutions at the time, opened a school in her own home.

In 1906, the family moved to Odessa, where Andrey worked for the Russian Maritime and Commercial Society (RMCS). Its offices were located on Deribasovskaya Street, named after the Marquis de Ribas, who helped build the city in the aftermath of the French Revolution. He built three buildings in Odessa which today are classified as protected monuments.

This large active port and cosmopolitan city had roads on a grid pattern with names such as "Greek Street" or "Armenian Street." It is especially famous for its grand staircase, which was immortalized by the film director Sergey Eisenstein in *The Battleship Potemkin*. Just as the people of Marseilles are known for their tall tales, so the people of Odessa are recognized for their mocking and detached way of viewing life. In a sort of secret code, their speech is woven with references that are totally obscure for the uninitiated. In a way it resembles Jewish humor, at once ebullient and tinged with melancholy. All your friends remember this humor as having colored your life, Dmitri. It's the first thing they mention about you—your eyes sparkling with mischief, a sense that you could be a good companion even during the saddest hours of your life.

# A Soaking Cat in Your Arms

∞ AT ODESSA YOUR FAMILY OCCUPIED A LARGE HOUSE RIGHT next to the sea on Lermontov Street, as if the poet himself had followed you from Pyatigorsk. The beach was very close, and your brother, your sister, and you often made use of it. One day, the Meyendorffs' dog next door chased your cat all the way to a cliff. Cornered and terrified, the poor animal had no choice but to jump into the water. You dove in after it and succeeded in bringing the cat back to the surface, now motionless and completely drenched. You ran back to the house sobbing, with the cat tightly pressed against your chest. Thankfully, the poor animal regained consciousness.

Nearly a century later, my daughter Svetlana encountered a very elderly man in New York who, upon learning that she was your granddaughter, tearfully recounted this episode of the soaked and disheveled cat which you held in your young arms. His name was Nikita Koulomzin. He was vacationing on the Black Sea coast and later ran into you while in Paris. He always kept the image of you as a compassionate child clutching a soaking cat in your arms.

You were sickly and weak and developed more slowly than other children your age. Thus you kept to a special diet, and as you were constantly being watched, you became passive and developed an inability to "be like others." Your grandmother closely guarded your diet. One day the chambermaid asked you if you would like some cocoa, to which you responded, "I don't know, ask my grandmother." Sometimes the feeling of powerlessness would throw you into a stubborn fit of rage. These fits, though, generally wouldn't last long, and you would quickly return to your daydreams. Nevertheless, very early on you displayed a great compassion for the weak and the bullied. Among your friends, one could count a number of children whom some considered "disfavored" by nature, and who upon interacting with you would suddenly become blissful as they seemed to forget their dissimilarities.

As we've seen, this compassion also extended to animals, which often attached themselves to you. You would playfully amuse yourself by sniffing the air like a dog or a cat. You did this so well, in fact, that certain domesticated animals would look at you cautiously, as if you had broken into their secret world.

From the beginning of your childhood you had a passion for horses. Later in life, wherever you were, you would be taken back to childhood as you smelled the odor of racing stables. In Serbia you enjoyed driving the carriage your father took to his work. Animals played a big role in your family, and you designated various members by animal names. Thus, you nicknamed your sister Tatiana "Lisitsa," the fox. Your aunt Anna was for her whole life referred to as the "Leopard." As for you, you were known as "Sobaka" the dog, the big clumsy doggie. This is how you would sign your name later on as you wrote to Mother while imprisoned at Compiègne. There is something about this symbol, the "totem," that seems especially tender and humble.

One summer day, as Anna Hippius recounts, you and your sister Tanya were playing in the garden with some other children. One of the boys about your same size and strength took a stick and began to destroy an ant hill. Seeing this, you ran and tried to take the stick from the boy's hands in order to help the ants. The two of you began to fight. The boy's brother rushed to join him, and both of them ganged up on you, who, in a sort of ecstasy, couldn't feel the blows raining down on you. Seeing this, Tanya jumped from the wall where she was sitting to help defend you. The fist fight soon turned into a general battle as the other children who were playing in the garden all joined in. Your sister returned to the house, her dress completely torn to shreds. Seeing her in this state, your mother asked what happened. Rather than reprimanding her, she simply sent her to change, saying that the matter would be examined during the school children's meeting.

I'll talk more about this school later on. Right now, however, it must be noted that the school children would usually meet every Thursday in order to review projects, make comments on their grades, and re-solve any possible conflicts. Sophia Klepinina attended these meetings only to make sure they went smoothly. It was the children who brought up problems and, if need be, found a way to correct the one at fault. This generally consisted in depriving him of playtime with the other children.

That Thursday, Sophia asked Tanya to recount the circumstances surrounding the fight. Tanya affirmed that she went to help her little brother, who was being beaten up by two boys, one of whom was bigger and stronger. The children judged Tanya's actions to be just. Sophia then asked one of the boys why he got involved in the battle. He an-swered, "I saw the others fighting so I did like everyone else." The jury decided that he had acted like a rascal and deserved to be suspended from playing for two days. Another boy replied, "I saw them fighting a girl and wanted to defend her." The jury considered that he had acted valiantly. This is how justice was practiced in your house on Lermon-tov Street.

The mercy you had for animals also extended to toys. You liked stuffed animals, and although you didn't play with them, you would take them with you to bed at night. Among them was a bear you espe-cially liked. One summer the entire family left for Switzerland on vaca-tion. On the train you and the rest of the children were sleeping when all of a sudden you let out a loud cry from your bunk. When ques-tioned, you explained that you were feeling sorry for your bear, which you had forgotten at home. In memory of this touching episode, Tanya kept that bear for a long time, even in exile. In Serbia, someone stole it. It was then her turn to cry.

# 'Pravda' Means Truth & Justice ☙

☙ BESIDES YOUR COMPASSION, THOSE CLOSE TO YOU REMEM-ber your sense of justice and truth. Your grandmother was rather suspicious of the ice cream sold on the street and thus forbade you children to buy it. One day you went for a walk with the coachman's son. Your passion for horses was so great that anything having to do with them made you overjoyed. During the walk, the coachman's son wanted ice cream and bought two servings at the first vendor he saw. Due to his participation in the sacred world of horses, you couldn't decline his offer, and so you ate your ice cream.

Upon returning home, you were overcome with an uneasy feeling and quickly went to see your grandmother. "Are we allowed to eat street vendor ice cream?" you asked, secretly hoping that this time she would say yes, or perhaps you lacked the courage to admit your disobedience to her point blank. Nonetheless, your grandmother responded very clearly: "No." You confessed to having eaten one. Seeing your sincerity, not only did she not punish you, but she didn't even have the heart to scold you. In many other cases, she would forgive you for things she wouldn't let the other children get away with.

Another episode related by Anna Hippius finely illustrates your cheerful character and the way you had distanced yourself from others. You children went for a long walk and took along a snack. As you were returning, you noticed a small piece of chocolate still in the sack and decided to draw lots. Maneuvers, calculations, trickery, and re-counting on everyone's part followed. You, however, stayed on the side-lines of these negotiations. Finally, they decided that the piece would be yours, then saw that the chocolate had disappeared. Without even blinking you pronounced, "It's swallowed." Amazed at this, the other children demanded, "What right did you have to eat that chocolate before we'd drawn lots?" To which you responded, "I calculated my-self that it would be mine." The calm and confident tone of your voice mixed with your honest reputation left the other children with gaping mouths.

This way of distancing yourself, this sort of absence from general discussions and raging disputes, occurred a number of times. One had the impression that you were deep in your universe and didn't no-tice what was happening around you. However, this didn't prevent you from discreetly observing conversations and at the right moment in-serting a response or amusing remark which would then serve to focus the general attention on you.

During some summers, your family would visit Europe. Around 1910, you rented a villa in Switzerland on the Four Districts Lake. It was here Sophia began a tradition to which you children became much attached. Each of you in turn would spend the night in your mother's room. In the early morning, you would go for a walk with her and dis-cuss the beauty of nature or whatever was on your heart. "They took pleasure in this intimacy with their mother," remembers Anna Hip-pius. "Discussion about God, love, and beauty weren't moral lessons for them, but a direct connection with reality; a reality which stayed in their memory and accompanied them for the rest of their lives."

Sophia made every attempt to take each of your personalities into consideration. It is most likely from this that the family tradition de-veloped of giving each child a nickname which distinguished him or her from every other Nikolai, Tatiana, and Dmitri in the area.

The Stepanov cousins were with you that year. Irina was the same age as you and had good memories of summers spent in Odessa and Swit-zerland. Her brother Alexander was also very close to you. In Odessa, they repainted a boat which they christened "Tinda," derived from the initials of all your first names.

# *God, Everywhere Present* ❧

❧ *I* SPOKE AT LENGTH WITH AUNT IRINA, WHO LIVED IN BOS-
ton. She told me a lot about your childhood in Russia. She had an interesting perspective regarding your family's religiosity which helped
me understand your spiritual evolution. "Our families were more theist
than Orthodox. We were steeped in the idea that God is everywhere—in
the starry sky, in the murmur of the sea, in our hearts—but we seldom
went to church. We didn't begin our meals with a prayer though during Holy Week we ate meagerly, and that more out of respect for con-
vention than moved by a true contrition. Despite all this, we took part
in religious instruction. Our parents insisted that we not be ignorant
and that Christian culture at least be a minimal part of our cultural
knowledge. However, our German housekeepers, generally either Lu-
theran or Catholic, would hang pious images above our beds, teach us
the Lord's Prayer in German, and pray with us for our parents and for
the unfortunate."

Your aunt Anna Hippius, who would later become so pious that one
would see her at the parish feast of every Russian Diaspora church in
Paris, notes in her posthumous biography of you, her dear "Dimka,"
that your family "was composed of people who loved God and all his
creatures."

You would, in fact, attend Holy Week services. You wrote in your
journal how a Holy Thursday service affected you. This all happened

in the "Orphanage Church" at the service when the twelve Gospels[1] are read. After each reading a bell rings, which indicates the number of pericopes completed. At the first reading, you turned toward your mother with a complicit smile. The softness of that smile and the expression of unity in prayer were so strong that several years later, this memory would come back to you. This time, you were in Constantinople attending the same service. You had been reluctant to go, but Sophia softly told you, "You felt so good at church back then, why do you fuss about going now?" The exapostilarion[2] about the good thief brought you to tears as you experienced the joy of repentance and the assurance of God's forgiveness.

Your godfather, the Christian intellectual Dmitri Merezhkovsky, concerned at the gulf forming between the Church and the Russian intelligentsia of that period, attempted to establish a bridge between the two groups. In 1901, he founded a philosophical and religious society in St. Petersburg and with much difficulty, obtained authorization from the Holy Synod (equivalent to the Ministry of Religion). However, the organization was dissolved a few years later following an edict from that same synod. His wife Zinaida Hippius notes that the clergy representatives and the intellectuals glared at each other in a hostile, stony silence; they weren't speaking a common language. Certain clerics even declared that a Christian culture is useless, because the liturgy by itself replaces all theological science. Thus everyone stood their ground on their opinions.

Nonetheless, your mother would read the Gospel and write prayers for you. Just before her death, when you were seventeen, she wrote a prayer for you in a notebook you kept your whole life.

> Father, accept the prayer of your children
> Visit them in secret; bless them and grant them a long life, health, joy
>     and a mutual love
> Send dew down upon the earthly vegetation

1   In the Orthodox Church, during matins of Holy Friday, which is usually celebrated on Thursday night, all the Gospel passages on the Passion of Christ are read, organized into twelve pericopes.
2   Hymn preceding the Praises after the matins canon: "O Lord, this very day hast Thou vouchsafed the Good Thief Paradise. By the Wood of the Cross do Thou enlighten me also and save me."

Fill our habitation with your silence and joy
Grant us, O Lord, perfect love free of every fear.
Amen.

This prayer, which you copied into your journal in 1929, would come to have an important role in your life—a life full of love and mercy for every creature.

Sophia, who was a trained educator, dedicated a lot of time to her children as she formed them to her world vision. In Odessa, she opened a model school in her own home, where she encouraged the creativity of the twenty pupils she had gathered. Together they composed a wall newspaper. As for you, at the age of five, even though you didn't know how to write, you came up with a Christmas story entitled "The Abandoned Christmas Tree." This was the story of a fir tree which, left in the attic after the holidays, slowly lost its needles as it became dejected in abandonment. No one came to scratch its back irritated by its dried-out needles. You would always have a sense of pity for the "small and forgotten," not excluding inanimate objects.

# Odessa in Torment ೞ

ೞ SEVERAL PROFESSORS FROM SOME OF ODESSA'S BEST EDU-cational institutions were invited to teach at the school on Lermontov Street. Every corner of the vast house was filled with groups of children occupied with their studies. Sophia took charge of catechism and tried to transmit both a living and traditional Orthodoxy to the students.

After completing studies at home, the boys entered high school. Your brother Nikolai was rather gifted and bright, while you had to struggle to climb the educational ladder. You were bad at self-organization and had to spend an insane amount of time doing homework. Alarmed by this, Sophia decided to have your vision checked. You went all the way to Kharkov and visited an eminent ophthalmologist, who prescribed glasses for you. All the same, you remained a mediocre student. So much for a classical education! You joined the *Realnoye Uchilishche*,[1] a secondary educational institution centered more on the sciences and technology than literary matters. At around fourteen years old, you had a sudden growth spurt and grew closer to the size a boy your age should be. You also played several sports, including rowing, bicycling, tennis, and swimming.

Your father Andrey was often absent due to his work on a number of construction sites. When the First World War broke out, it became a duty to enlist in the motherland's army. Even though Nikolai was too

---

1   A secondary educational institution in Tsarist Russia where the natural sciences and applied mathematics took precedence over literary subjects.

young to be called up to battle, he became restless and joined the Volunteer Army[2] two years later. Sophia became one of Russia's rare female justices of the peace. With this title, she became busy with social action and visitation of Odessa's more disadvantaged areas. This position would later save her life. In 1919, with her husband far away in Novorossiisk, the civil war reached the southern regions of Russia, and Sophia was arrested and incarcerated by the Bolsheviks. A few weeks later a young Jewish revolutionary stepped in on her behalf. As justice of the peace, Sophia had defended this man after he was arrested by the tsarist police for distributing tracts.

Sophia's arrest left the family completely helpless. It greatly affected you and served as the impetus for you to spontaneously enter a church for the first time at fourteen years old. This first encounter ended in failure. Apprehensive, you entered an enclosed women's monastery as a service was taking place. Unfamiliar with the customs, you stood in the middle of the faithful with your hands behind your back. When one of the nuns approached and admonished you for this, you left the convent feeling sad and helpless. Anna Hippius notes, "Having such a sensitive character, this formal and indelicate correction was enough to isolate him from the church for a long time."

In the summer of 1919, Odessa was retaken by the White Army's[3] Volunteer Corps. Life came back to normal, though interwoven with fear. Your brother Nikolai fought in the army of General Wrangel.[4] Since you were too young for the army, you took a job as a ship boy in a commercial fleet which was a dependency of your father's employer and was traveling across the Black Sea. The crew took you on with affection, and certain sailors remembered you, saying, "Why, it's none other than Dimka!" They associated the memory of you with one especially

2   At the beginning of the First World War, the Russian Army was composed not only of a professional military but also included very young volunteer corps. The latter would subsequently play a determining role in the composition of the White Army, which later came up against the revolutionaries organized as the Red Army by Trotsky. The Red Army and the White Army would fight violently against one another throughout the civil war.

3   For two straight years, the entire Russian South passed from one ruling power to another, each group rivaling the other in violence and leaving countless numbers of victims.

4   The well-known figure General Wrangel (1878–1928) led the White Army on the southern front.

joyful time when you and they had decided to dive from the top of a cliff[5] into the sea.

Odessa was retaken by the Red Army. The punishments again affected the nobility, to which your family belonged. The writer Ivan Bunin, in his book *Cursed Days,*[6] evokes the chaotic atmosphere that ruled in 1919 Odessa. Under Bolshevik rule both arrests and summary executions increased while bands of armed anarchists organized massacres in the surrounding areas. The peasants were not left any supplies, and famine ensued. Communication was cut off from the rest of the country, where the civil war was raging.

You rejoined your family, who had fled to Constantinople. It was the first stage in a life of exile. Most emigrants regarded this exile as only temporary. They had an immense hope that the Bolsheviks would quickly fall from power so they would be able to return to their country.

---

5   See Sergey Zhaba's "Recollections" (in Russian) in *Vestnik* (the RSCM newsletter), No. 131, Paris, 1980, pp. 333–341.
6   Ivan Bunin, *Cursed Days. A Diary of Revolution,* Chicago 1998.

# ❦ III ❦

# *In Exile: Constantinople to Belgrade*

# From Constantinople
# to Belgrade ∞

∞ THE KLEPININS TOOK ONLY A FEW SUITCASES WITH THEM, one of which contained identification papers and jewelry and was thus nicknamed "the apple of my eye." Along with their German governess and other family friends, they crammed themselves into a three-storied Turkish building which they designated "the Starling's Nest." You and Irina entered the American college (Robert's College) where you pursued a secondary education.

It was with great pleasure that I read *Beg* (*The Race*). This play by Mikhail Bulgakov describes the disorder of Southern Russia at that time and sets one act in Constantinople. Near the end of the war of 1914–18, the city was an occupied zone. The British marines, impeccable in dress and behavior, stood right next to the French soldiers from the expeditionary forces. They felt nothing but contempt for the Russian émigrés who had brought with them only a few suitcases filled with their former magnificence, and who now found themselves reduced to selling even the buttons from their uniforms. France had generously ceded Gallipoli Island, beyond the Bosporus, to the Russian military. However, the civilians had all the trouble in the world finding jobs and places to live.

While your father Andrey looked to renew his contacts with the Maritime Transportation Society, ROPIT, which had employed him in Russia, Sophia hurried back to Yalta to assist your brother Nikolai, who had contracted typhus. The Crimea was, in fact, benefiting from a reprieve when, on February 9, 1918, Germany signed a separate peace agreement with the Ukrainian Council, which had asked for protection from Russia. Anticipating the Brest-Litovsk[1] agreements, the Germans occupied Ukraine, holding off the Reds. Moreover, the British squadron, desiring to protect the aged and wealthy Empress Maria, a refugee in the summer residence of the deposed emperor, anchored off the shore of Sebastopol. Sophia successfully saved Nikolai, but learned that her own brother, Vasily Stepanov, had just died from a heart attack following a sudden evacuation from Constantinople to Paris. This was too much for her, and she began to feel the onset of angina pectoris. As the Revolution took off on their own turf,[2] the Germans left the Crimea, which was then immediately occupied by the Red Army. There was a general evacuation. The English and French navies left Russia and packed even the ship holds full of leading aristocrats, military personnel, and other state employees. All were expressly forbidden to bring more than two trunks per family.

In Constantinople, the housing and work crisis was acute. The family had to look somewhere else. Sophia finally learned that your father had an opportunity for employment in Serbia with the Standard Oil Company. King Alexander was very generous towards Russians, who had fought to protect the kingdom of Serbia.[3] Moreover, Sophia was convinced that the Bolsheviks were doomed to fall. Serbia seemed like a sunny country, likeable, Slavic, not to mention Orthodox, a place where the children could study while waiting for Russia to be liberated from communism. Thus, in 1921 you and your family emigrated to Serbia. You settled in Belgrade, where you made friends with the Zernov, Lopukhin, and Troyanov families. They too were refugees in

1   The Brest-Litovsk Agreements (March 3, 1918) were negotiated by Lenin as a separate peace agreement with exorbitant financial and territorial conditions. Russia notably abandoned Ukraine, which would fall victim to armed mobs and bands of anarchists.

2   In November 1918, groups of soldiers and workers, encouraged by the Spartakists, attempted to begin a revolution in Germany. A provisional government suppressed the insurrections. On August 11, 1919, a republican constitution was adopted, putting an end to the rule of the Habsburg Dynasty.

3   King Alexander (1888–1934) was sympathetic towards Russia, where he had studied. He was very generous toward Russian refugees, awarding scholarships to students and authorizing the opening of emigrant associations. Russian officers were able to continue to wear their uniforms and participate in military parades and drills.

the Serbian capital. Thus were formed the first close bonds that would characterize the Russian Orthodox environment of the Diaspora, something that would be passed on even to the third generation of children.

During my adolescence in Paris, I had the opportunity to become well acquainted with the Zernovs. Sophia, the eldest, greatly impressed me. She was a first-class lady and always elegant. She had opened her own social assistance office and collaborated with Mother Maria Skobtsova. She could also often be seen at Lourmel. My mother told me that, unlike Mother Maria, Sophia Zernova felt a certain repulsion towards the homeless, who might come in a little too drunk or slovenly for her taste. The poor men would suddenly become quite self-conscious as they tried to present themselves to her in a dignified manner. "No, Sophia Mikhaylovna," stammered one of them one day, "you are wrong to say that I smell of alcohol. I just finished eating a mandarin orange." All of Lourmel was amused by this reply and began to nickname drunken people "mandarin eaters."

In Paris, we would also frequent the good and gentle doctor Vladimir Zernov, whose office was often visited by the Russian community of the Fifteenth Arrondissement. We would meet him and his family at the church on Olivier de Serres Street. He was the person who delivered certificates of good health to the RSCM's summer camps. As for Nicolas Zernov and his wife Militsa, who lived in Oxford, they participated in RSCM conferences, where they would often speak. A few times, Maria and her husband Gustav Kullman,[4] the last of the Zernovs, would come from Switzerland. The Zernovs gave everyone the comforting impression of a real Christian family, active in the Church, calm and joyful, lacking all ostentation.[5]

4  Doctor of Law at the University of Berne, infatuated with Russian culture, Gustav Kullmann (1894–1961) was very interested in Orthodoxy. In his capacity of secretary of the YMCA among the Russian refugees in Germany, he helped hundreds of students, financed Nikolai Berdyaev's revue *Put'*, and contributed to the creation of the publishing house YMCA-Press, where the majority of books from the "Paris School" of theology and philosophy were edited. Having married Maria Zernova and become Orthodox, he often spoke about Orthodoxy at ecumenical conferences. He held high positions in the Refugee Commission of the League of Nations.

5  See the history of the Zernov family (in Russian): *Khronika sem'i Zernovykh; Za Rubezhom,* Belgrade, Paris, Oxford, YMCA-Press, 1973. Combining my own memories with what they published, I will largely use the Zernovs' testimony as a source for the Serbian years of Fr. Dimitri's youth.

# *The Ark Circle* ೮೪

ೞ Baptized "The Ark" in 1920, the Zernovs' Belgrade home became a meeting place for Russian youth residing in Serbia. Inspired by Nicolas Zernov, who had studied theology, an Orthodox student circle formed, and friendships came about. The young Olga Verigina, who was one year older than you, wrote this in her personal journal: "Nicolas Zernov spoke about civic-mindedness, and Nikolai Klepinin retold the legend of St. Nicholas and St. Cassian. . . . Yes, while helping others, we shouldn't be afraid of getting dirty. . . . During a pause, Dima Klepinin passed me a note telling me that my leaving made him sad because he wanted us to be friends. He's a nice boy, so I promised to write him from France." You must have made some rather awkward advances toward the beautiful Olga, and then she suddenly up and left. You hardly had any success in your attempts with young women.[1]

The circle was exceptional for the powerful faith of the young Russians attending it. This faith had been rediscovered in a foreign land which, in an interesting paradox, was also an Orthodox monarchy. Forced into exile, these young people appeared to be searching for their identity and specific role in a renewed vision of the Orthodox faith. Until then they had considered this faith to be a quasi-inseparable attribute of the imperial monarchy, which had now been replaced by an

---

1  See Olga Verigina-Mozhayskaya, *Journal* (in Russian), excerpt from the Mozhaysky family archives.

atheistic Soviet state. This circle organized as a sort of fraternity, a brotherhood which placed itself under the protection of St. Seraphim of Sarov. As Nicolas Zernov noted, the group's particular goal included building a bridge between the pre-revolutionary generation and the young Orthodox who had come to a conscious faith after 1917.

Like these young people, you, Dima, were seeking to understand what brought about the Revolution's success, the collapse of the ancient world, and your exile. The circle's discussions focused on historical problems as much as they did on theology, philosophy, and esthetics. Discussion took place concerning the role that both the East and West played in forming Russian identity. The everlasting enmity between Slavophiles and Westerners suddenly became very real. Nicolas Zernov had the opportunity to attend the first bishops' conference at Sremsky-Karlovtsy in 1921,[2] and subsequently the role of the Church also appeared in a new light. He explained indignantly how political interests had taken precedence over spiritual questions and how the conference ended by stamping out any vague attempts made by the Russian Diaspora to reorganize ecclesiastical life.

Here, in Belgrade, the young Russians wanted to find in the Church—by way of an active parish life—the "rare pearl" for which they were ready to sacrifice other values, such as material well-being and social privilege. The themes tackled in the group meetings finely illustrated a newness and diversity of interests. Nicolas Zernov cited a number of such topics, including "Asceticism in the World," "Monarchy," "Christianity and Art," "Bolshevism," "The Role of Women in the Church," "The Dangers of Smoking," "Divine Providence," and "The Meaning of the Four Gospels."

A number of eminent theologians were invited to the Zernovs' modest home. These included people such as Basil Zenkovsky,[3] who had

---

2 Gathered together in the Serbian patriarch's residence at the request of Metropolitan Anthony Khrapovitsky (1863–1936), who would become leader of the Russian Orthodox Church Outside Russia, the delegates voted on motions for the reestablishment of the monarchy and an appeal to Western powers to break contact with the Bolsheviks. A part of the delegates assembled around Archbishop Benjamin Fedchenko expressed their disappointment at not having had the opportunity to address the questions relating to the Church.

3 Educator, psychologist, and historian of Russian philosophy Basil Zenkovsky (1881–1962) played a large role in the creation of the RSCM, of which he was president. Having emigrated to France, he taught at the St. Sergius Institute    *(cont.)*

been Minister of Religion in Kiev as well as a vigorous defender of the faith. His first lecture, entitled, "The Causes of the Russian Revolution," constituted an entire program in which he made the bold claim that one of the main causes was the smothering of religious thought by the autocracy.

Another great speaker, Sergey Bezobrazov,[4] the future Bishop Cassian, who had just escaped the Bolshevik prisons, also insisted on spiritual freedom, without which the Church wouldn't be able to fulfill her mission in a secularized world.

The leader of the "Karlovites," Metropolitan Anthony Khrapovitsky, was invited more than once to the Ark Circle. He had a particular charisma for the youth, whom he encouraged to serve the Church without servility. In spite of some rather reactionary political positions, he defended the vision of a very dynamic Church, particularly denouncing the sycophancy of the "Church chamberlains" he had known in Imperial Russia.

As a sign of the open atmosphere that would come to characterize the future RSCM, one issue among others in the Belgrade group came up when the youth invited Bishop (now Saint) Nikolai Velimirovich, the "Serbian Chrysostom." With all simplicity, he came to their modest meeting place in the Belgrade suburbs and by his ardent faith communicated to the young Russians his hope that the Russian Church would quickly emerge victorious from the trials it was then experiencing, and that it would assist the Christian world in returning to the apostolic tradition.

Basil Zenkovsky remembered your arrival in the philosophical-religious circle. He already knew you since he had frequently visited your parents.[5] As a professional psychologist, he described you rather meticulously: "He was between sixteen and seventeen years old, but looked much younger than his age; his thinking was slow. However, he made an extraordinarily agreeable impression, for he was a nice boy,

of Orthodox Theology. Strongly encouraged by his former student Dimitri, he became a priest in 1942.

4   An eminent specialist and New Testament translator, Sergey Bezobrazov (1892–1965) taught in particular at the St. Sergius Institute of Orthodox Theology.

5   Each time he finished a job, Andrey Klepinin would come back to Belgrade and joyfully meet with members of the Ark Circle. Since these people wanted to have their own church and launched a campaign for one, he built a church called the Russian Church of Belgrade.

a timid little twig; not very talkative, but basically good, modest and sincere."

Zenkovsky left for Prague in the spring of 1923 but remained in contact with the Belgrade youth. You also had corresponded with him, as he mentions here:

> I remember his writing which was a bit gauche with disproportionate handwriting. His letters were always short, but surprisingly consistent. He never expressed typical things, but would confide two or three of his thoughts and emotions. It was always so profound, so unexpected, and so authentic—because it came from deep down within him. His letters stood out from all the others and are engraved in my memory.[6]

In contact with the youth from the Belgrade circle, you felt that you were liked. As your Aunt Hippius describes, "Dmitri found in these youth an authentically Christian setting associated with the Church, something his heart had long hoped for. It was within this embrace that his definitive encounter with life in the Church would occur."[7]

---

6  This description by Professor Basil Zenkovsky is a posthumous homage. It was delivered during a soirée dedicated to the memory of Father Dimitri Klepinin and published in Russian, in Paris, in the bulletin number 2 of *Vestnik Tserkovnoj Zhizni*, March 15, 1945.
7  Journal of Anna Hippius, manuscript in Russian, H.K.A. archives.

# *Opening to Ecumenical Dialogue*

WHETHER SERBIAN OR RUSSIAN ORTHODOX, EVERYONE felt at home in the Ark Circle. That is, up until the day when an unknown American asked by telephone for permission to attend a meeting. His name was Ralph Hollinger and he represented the Young Men's Christian Association, the famous YMCA. The young Orthodox were amazed by this request. Nicolas Zernov and his companions considered Western Christians as heretics. As for the YMCA, with its Masonic triangle, it was considered nothing less than an enemy of the Church. What could they do? In spite of this, they decided to invite Ralph Hollinger, determined to argue with him. Instead they met a man with a good knowledge of both the Russian language and Orthodoxy, who ended up making an excellent impression on the majority of the members. Certain people, however, left the circle, accusing the Zernovs of dealing with the devil.

The Orthodox youth's opening to Western Christianity would be affirmed little by little. Soon a representative for the World Student Christian Federation, Alexander Nikitin, sent a letter inviting Belgrade circle members to a series of international student conferences. Once again they hesitated as to whether or not to accept subsidies from unknown Western organizations. However, curiosity induced them to discover other ways of celebrating and living their faith. They decided to send a delegation to a conference in Budapest, with the mission of reporting back to the circle on whether or not cooperation with non-Orthodox movements would be useful.

Here we find the beginnings of the ecumenical movement as it occurred in the twentieth century. The Orthodox Diaspora would divide into two camps according to their attitude concerning relationships between Christians.

In 1923, Basil Zenkovsky, Sergey Bezobrazov, and Sophia Zernova returned from the Hungarian capital full of enthusiasm. Apart from a few Romanians, they had been the sole Orthodox in the midst of a sea of Protestants. No one knew a thing about Orthodoxy, nor about the persecution of Russian Christians. The Russians had been the focus of an immense and sincere interest and felt like missionaries for Orthodoxy. As a result of this, missions in the West would multiply.

Nicolas Zernov and your brother Nikolai left for England in order to attend a British Student Christian Movement (BSCM) conference. As they were both stateless, they had to maneuver quite a bit in order to obtain travel visas from Serbia. In order to do this, they played on prejudices against that "treacherous Albion" who had left the White Army during the civil war. They wanted to verify that they could trust all of these Protestants who were interested in them and to see if they were of good faith.

The two Nicholases traveled by train through Austria, Germany, and France. In Vienna, they rushed to visit the city and bought some clothes in order to be a bit more presentable in front of the Westerners. They marveled before St. Stephan's Cathedral. "It was my first encounter with Gothic," exclaimed Nicolas Zernov. Your brother was already familiar with those things since your mother had often taken you to Western Europe. However, he was still dumbfounded by the well-being of Europeans, a culture with which he had lost acquaintance during the last ten years of war and revolution, marked by a long recovery from typhus and a quick escape with only a few bags. Laughing, he told Zernov how they had been afraid of losing the famous bag filled with precious objects which they had nicknamed the "apple of their eyes."

There was much disenchantment in Munich as France had just occupied the Ruhr. Dumbfounded, the two Nicholases witnessed a menacing military demonstration punctuated with anti-French slogans.[1]

---

1   Humiliated by the Treaty of Versailles (1919) and the loss of Alsace-Lorraine, the Germans did not hide their anti-French sentiments, which were exacerbated when France occupied the Ruhr.

Russian friends lodged them in Paris and invited them to a French cancan show at Montmartre. Zernov was rather put off by this and preferred to slip away to visit the basilica of Sacré-Cœur, where he emotionally observed as Parisians venerated the Holy Sacrament. Exhausted by a several-hour-long marathon through the Louvre and Notre Dame, they caught a train to Calais. The way they were received in Dover was awful. Their papers from Serbia seemed questionable, and they were interrogated regarding both their origin and the purpose of their trip. Thankfully, your brother spoke English, though he still felt like a social outcast, like one of the emigrants that they might turn back. They ended up obtaining the authorization to continue their trip to Derbyshire, where they stayed for ten days, from the twentieth to the thirtieth of July, 1928, at the interconfessional conference which brought together not only Anglicans but also Protestants from a diverse number of denominations.

Zernov gave a rather amusing description of the young English, Irish, and Pakistani Christians attending. What especially struck him was their extremely youthful character and relaxed and informal approach toward their bishops and pastors. Even though he was of about the same age as they, he had recently lived through some very tragic events since the Revolution, and felt more mature than these British people who were wearing shorts. Moreover, he had the habit of respecting bishops. He sat dumbfounded as he attended the improvised speech of an Anglican bishop, who was barely recognizable in his "dog collar" and, perched on a seat, provoked laughter from the congregation with one-liners. However, as Zernov didn't know much English, he was distrustful both of the speech's content and of the prayers. There was always that same fear of heretics!

One night, Zernov argued about it with your brother, who was more comfortable and familiar with Protestants. A colony of German Lutherans had settled in Odessa, where the Klepinin family used to rent a dacha during the summer months. Your German Catholic nanny, "Fräulein," not only lived with you kids, but even followed you to Serbia. It was from her that you learned to recite the "Our Father," or "*Vater Unser*," before going to bed. You were the Benjamin, Fräulein's favorite. When she was dying, the news reached you in Paris, where you were studying theology at the St. Sergius Institute, and you quickly returned to Serbia. You would learn that, impressed by your priestly vocation, she had long since converted to Orthodoxy. She would die in your arms.

At first, Nicolas Zernov asked your brother to refrain from praying anything but the "Our Father" with the Anglicans. Then he realized that he would have to deal with Christians who were just as sincere as he. At the end of the ten days, through discussion with various people, he confessed that he had fallen under the charm of the British youth, who had such profound belief and such authentic demeanors. He promised himself to look deeper at the dogmatic differences separating Christians of various confessions and to search for a common ground with his Protestant companions.

# *Sophia's Death* ঙઉ

ঙઉ $A$PART FROM THESE MISSIONS TO FOREIGN COUNTRIES, the circle's meetings and the church services, these young Russians in Serbia benefited from a spiritual center of primary importance: the Monastery of Hopovo. The priest Fr. Alexis Nelyubov served at this monastery and would come to play a significant role in your spiritual development.

Sisters gathered at Hopovo who, during the 1914 war, had been driven from the Lesna convent founded by Mother Catherine. Born Countess Efimovskaya, this remarkable woman took up the monastic vocation, "not in order to flee the world, but in order to transfigure it." She worked to make it possible for nuns to obtain a formation in theology,[1] and she favored reestablishing the order of deaconess. At Hopovo she continued to gather orphans just as she had in Lesna. She confessed that she did not accept the idea of eternal suffering for one's sins, which in her eyes contradicted the immeasurable love of God. To get to Mother Catherine's convent, one had to travel some seventy kilometers by train to Ruma, then walk another eighteen kilometers on Mount Frushka's forested paths in the territory of the former Austro-Hungarian Empire.

In his memoirs, Zernov describes Father Alexis as severe but soft, attentive in loving his spiritual children, knowing how to share both

---

1   Nikolai Klepinin left his memoirs (in Russian) about this Mother Catherine: *Pamyati igumeni Yekateriny,* Paris, 1926.

their joys and their pain. "He instructed us, consoled us, forgave us, and prayed to God for us," noted Sophia Zernova. You made him your confessor and even went so far as to give him your journal, where you wrote this note to him:

Dear Father Alexis,

[. . .] At first I was displeased with my journal and it even disgusted me, but I would like you to read it so that you may know even my slightest thoughts. I don't want to hide anything from you.

The priest replied to you with this note:

Dear Dima,

I skimmed through your journal too quickly to give you a detailed opinion. Don't be ashamed of the first pages. You have to learn how to experience everything because only what is dear to us can become even more dear. May you go on with God's help. I embrace you.

Your Father, Alexis Nelyubov

It was in another monastery, this one opened by Metropolitan Benjamin Fedchenko, that you came to have a decisive experience that one might even describe as "mystical." With great self-restraint you remember it in your journal. One day as you were on your way to the monastery, you got lost and night overtook you. You decided to sleep in the woods and buried yourself in a pile of dead leaves under a sort of improvised hut. In the first glow of dawn, you caught sight of the monastery's domes, from which a light sound of ringing bells reached you. At that moment you felt sure of the presence of God in your life. Later on, in moments of doubt and despair, the evoking of this aurora—that of a never-waning light—would help you to overcome your anguish.

In the summer the Klepinins shared a villa with a Russian woman whose son was a musician and who had been born blind. I had the opportunity to meet him thirty years later. I had just been employed as a teacher of Russian in Le Mans when Father Igor Vernik pointed out to me that one of his parishioners lived in that town in a community for the blind. I visited him and found that he really was that same famous Mikhail Fedorov, the musician from the Belgrade suburbs. He remembered my family well and also remembered my grandmother's funeral, which had been attended by the entire Russian community.

On Saturday, February 24, 1923, your mother slowly faded after having been so happy to see everyone reunited. You were with your brother at the vigil service. Your father Andrey had just quickly returned from the Bor mining factory on the Dalmatian coast. Your sister Tatiana, alarmed by your mother's condition, returned from Prague after having been there a while studying dance with the choreographer Emile-Jacques Dalcroze. Andrey stood on the balcony to watch for your return from church. "Mama's gone," he told you, as soon as he caught sight of you.

This death brought you even closer to Christ as Consoler. Father Alexis Nelyubov took your mourning to heart and helped you to accept this death as a Christian. You would receive a lot of support from family friends during those days.

Professor Basil Zenkovsky remembers Sophia's death. He notes that in addition to this loss, something very important had just broken in this "solid and cultivated" family.

Your mother continued to accompany you on your spiritual journey even beyond her death, as you wrote seven years later to a close friend, Sophia Shidlovskaya:

> The day I realized that all I've ever wished for in my life is distant from me was the first time I understood the significance of suffering [. . .] But joy came back to me when I remembered the Savior's words: "Come to me, all who labor and are heavy laden, and I will give you rest. Take my yoke upon you and learn from me; for I am gentle and lowly in heart and you will find rest for your souls. For my yoke is easy, and my burden is light."[2] I had come to my mother's grave with the heavy burden of worldly worries. Everything seemed confused and unsolvable when suddenly I found the light yoke of Christ. I've never known a day more joyful than that day and I thank God for all he's given me to bear. After that experience, I reoriented my life and it became easier to resolve certain problems.[3]

Your personal journals are full of tenderness for your departed mother. At twenty-five years of age, you received a scholarship to study

2   Matthew 11:28–30.
3   Letter to Sophia Shidlovskaya. Manuscript in Russian, H.K.A. archives.

theology at the General Theological Seminary in New York. While on the open sea en route to the United States, the seventeenth of September 1929, you wrote:

Dear Mother,

It's your feast today and I wish I could be with you. I reread your letters and it's a little as though I've responded to you. If God wills, I'll be in New York tomorrow morning. A new chapter of my life is about to open. Thanks to your letters, I once again sense how much you participate in my whole life. Even now you remain with me. Not long ago, conscious of what was awaiting me and what I should do with my life, your love helped shape my future. The same goes for today: you see further and more clearly down the road which is still hidden to my eyes. If you have this privilege of being close to God, help me to follow the path that is acceptable to Him.

I'm so happy that you know that I love you and that despite my blindness and my lack of attention towards you, you feel my love. I'm going to sleep, but you, stay with me like before, when I was along the Bosporus and you were in Yalta. God willing, I'll write again.

Memory Eternal!

Five months later, on the eighth anniversary of Sophia's death, as you were still in the United States where you were studying St. Paul, you continued to feel as if she were watching and guiding you.

It's already been eight years . . . and I'm in America. Where will I be on the ninth anniversary? My God! Have mercy on me a sinner! She sees my entire life and my impurity. Lord, help me during this year to praise You with a pure heart and to fittingly implore You to grant her eternal rest.

# The Russian Student
# Christian Movement ∞

∞ SOME MONTHS AFTER YOUR MOTHER'S DEATH, AN IMPOR-
tant event occurred which brought the Belgrade circle's members together and gave them new life. Between the first and the eighth of October, 1923, an international conference of Russian student groups was
held in Pserov, Czechoslovakia. Your circle sent four delegates: Sophia
and Nicolas Zernov, Professor Sergey Bezobrazov, as well as the Ark's
columnist, Ivan Rastorguyev.

About thirty Russians came from the four corners of Europe and assembled in an ancient Habsburg hunting pavilion. They were joined by
some Americans, including Ralph Hollinger, a handful of British people, and a Swiss man, Gustav Kullman, who afterwards would become
Orthodox and marry Maria Zernova. The goal was to get to know one
another in order to exchange experiences and attempt to resuscitate
the Christian movement of students who had been born in Russia but
then had been swept away by the October Revolution.

Several of the movement's founders organized this rally. These included Lev Liperovsky, who, later in Paris when you were both priests,
would become a close friend; Alexander Nikitin, who helped to start
the Belgrade circle; Vladimir Martsinkovsky, who, born in Russia,
was a disciple of Baron Nicholai,[1] the founder of the biblical and

---

1  The Protestant preacher Baron Nicholai (1863–1919) was the initiator of Bible study
groups in Russia which brought together Protestants and Orthodox.

philosophical studies group *Mayak* (the lighthouse)[2] in St. Petersburg.

However, the presence of several Christian philosophers who had recently been expelled from the USSR would contribute to the success and weight of this first assembly in Pserov. These included Fr. Sergius Bulgakov,[3] the philosopher Nikolai Berdyaev (1878–1948), as well as the elderly and respected professor Paul Novgorodtsev (1866–1924), a philosopher, sociologist, and lawyer. At the beginning of the conference they all felt like foreigners in the midst of these young émigrés. A number of professors also came to the conference, including Basil Zenkovsky, the Church historian Anton Kartashev (1875–1960), the archpriest and theologian George Florovsky (1893–1979), and the philosopher Leon Zander (1893–1964), who would play a dominant role in the birth of the RSCM.

This founding meeting would seem miraculous to future generations—a providential nudge in the right direction. But if one were to believe Nicolas Zernov's report,[4] the movement was far from guaranteed success. The participants distrusted the organizers, and just as when Ralph Hollinger visited Belgrade, certain people suspected the Protestants of being Freemasons on a mission to harm Orthodoxy. Others held a negative view of the professors who had been expelled from the USSR, reproaching them for their Marxist past and holding them responsible for the catastrophe in Russia. As for the objective of the student circles, opinions diverged. On one hand, those who attended the Bible study groups had only one goal in mind—to convert nonbelievers to the faith, regardless of their participation in the life of any particular church. On the other hand, the Belgrade group primarily envisioned its activity only within the Orthodox Church. Consequently, from the outset it had been surrounded by priests and theologians and always consulted with the bishops. For its members, a Christianity that was not anchored in the Church was an absurdity.

---

2  Inspired by their Protestant brethren, certain Orthodox such as Lev Liperovsky would in turn found Bible study groups more focused on the sacramental life of the Church.

3  The eminent philosopher and inspired theologian Fr. Sergius Bulgakov (1871–1944) is the author of a number of works, such as *The Orthodox Church* and *The Unwaning Light,* some of which have been published in English. A founder of the RSCM and the spiritual father of a number of its members, he also was the first dean of the St. Sergius Institute, where he enkindled many vocations.

4  Zernov, op. cit., ch. 14, pp. 87–106.

Nonetheless, people were all curious to meet one another, and the first night was very animated. They were all seeking to learn about each others' experiences, to develop a sense of communion, and to let a consensus emerge. That night, the rumor spread that Fr. Sergius Bulgakov would celebrate the Liturgy at dawn.

To everyone's general surprise, all of the attendees participated. This was the beginning of a miracle, as the ex-Marxist turned priest and theologian celebrated in such an inspiring way that everything else came together by itself. The participants felt like members of a single body. Both young and elderly, old emigrants and newcomers, monarchists and democrats, all felt as if they were engaged in a common task. The Protestants also appreciated the power of this Liturgy and united themselves spiritually to the Orthodox.

They decided to begin each day with the Liturgy, and thus this nascent movement anchored itself in the sacramental life. Common prayer, lectures, animated discussion, the pursuit of practical solutions for attracting young exiled Russians to the faith, all helped to create an atmosphere of friendship and trust. With one voice it was decided to found the Russian Student Christian Movement (RSCM). Basil Zenkovsky, who was familiar with the circles in both Prague and Belgrade and who worked tirelessly in Pserov, was elected president, and Liperovsky was elected general secretary.

While waiting for the second congress, a "coordination board of European student circles" was elected whose main office would be in Prague. The expression "the ecclesialization of life" became the movement's slogan. This emphasized the fact that Christianity isn't solely a religion of personal salvation but a force destined to transfigure every aspect of life. Especially present at the conference was the image of a suffering Russia delivered up to the godless Bolsheviks who, by way of terror and violence, attempted to establish an "earthly paradise" on the ruins of the old world. The participants prayed to God that He would grant them the grace to struggle for the restoration of the image of a Christianity that would transfigure the world.

Professor Kartashev, who had been the last procurator of the Holy Synod and the first head of the Ministry of Religion under Kerensky,[5] made a profound impression on the participants by encouraging them

5   Before emigrating the following year, Alexander Kerensky (1893–1970) presided over Russia's provisional government in 1917.

to rethink the idea of an authentically Christian society. It was given to Fr. Sergius Bulgakov to speak the final word: "Not long ago in the Church, everything was provided for and we could remain passive. From now on, history requires us to be active and inventive and to search out new reforms of ecclesial life that pertain to all Christians." He called for the members of the RSCM to declare themselves responsible for the fate of the Church both in Russia and in exile; to understand that the Eucharist is the cornerstone of life; and to seize the universality of Orthodoxy, which needed to open itself to other Christian confessions. "Don't be afraid," he concluded, "'because, as St. Paul says, 'I can do all things through Christ who strengthens me.'"

The conference ended on a Sunday, and all of the Orthodox present received communion. The blissful feeling of this mystical union revealed itself as so powerful that no one wanted to leave the room. In a moment of inspiration, Liperovsky suddenly intoned the Paschal Troparion, and in the Habsburg manor house there resounded the triumphant hymn, "Christ is risen from the dead."

The conference participants enthusiastically returned to Belgrade. As for you, you became enflamed with the idea of doing something useful with your life. Why not study theology like Nicolas Zernov?

When the time came, you participated in the Hopovo conference organized by the tireless Zernovs. You wrote in your notebook:

> What a great day in my life. I'm beginning to learn about such important things which could completely change my whole life. My God, see to it that this may be so.

You began to cherish the idea of dedicating your life to God. From that point on, you copied thoughts down in your journal along with prayers and writings from Fr. John of Kronstadt,[6] whose great deeds were gaining renown and who would be canonized half a century later. The Belgrade circle's conferences on St. Seraphim of Sarov inspired you to write rules for yourself in red, though you soon became distressed

---

6  Canonized in 1990 by the Moscow Patriarchate, John of Kronstadt (1829–1908) is one of the major figures of Russian spirituality, who manifested with a rare intensity the unity between the sacrament of the altar and the sacrament of brotherhood, life of prayer and social engagement. He is the author of a remarkable journal: *My Life in Christ*.

when you could not follow them. The first of December, 1923, as you reflected on death you solemnly noted:

> After my death, which may come unexpectedly, I would like for all of my possessions to be distributed to the poor, down to the last objects and for my name to be inscribed on the Church diptychs so that at each Liturgy the bloodless sacrifice will be celebrated for me.

Your brother also thought about studying theology. He had in mind above all the fate of Russia. Then he got married and had to find some lucrative work. Your sister Tatiana married a certain Borel who frequented the Ark meetings with his sister. She would eventually leave for Prague in order to teach dance lessons. Your father found a steady job in the Bor mines and, after Sophia's death, decided to settle there. "Fräulein" would look after him, and the house would be empty.

A theological institute dedicated to St. Sergius had just opened in Paris. You already knew most of its professors, such as Zenkovsky, Bezobrazov, along with the dynamic Archbishop Benjamin (Fedchenko). Fräulein said with a smile, "The last of the young ones is going to forget the German I taught him when he's in the midst of the French!" But she was proud that her Dima wanted to be a priest.

Materially, the situation wasn't very clear. The students at St. Sergius would live on campus and receive a small stipend. Would it be enough? Andrey promised to send money, and autumn was spent preparing and obtaining a visa. "Nansen"[7] was written on yours, and in the section denoting nationality the stamp simply said, "Stateless."

---

7 In 1922, the Nobel Peace Prize winner and Norwegian explorer Fridtjof Nansen (1861–1930) launched an initiative for displaced persons to carry an identity card called the Nansen Passports. After his death in 1931, the Nansen Bureau was formed in Geneva for refugees, notably White Russians, Armenians from Turkey, and later, German Jews.

# ❧ IV ❧

# *Theological Formation*

# Crimea Street, Paris ✣

✣ *P*ARIS SEEMED COLD AND UNWELCOMING TO YOU AFTER Serbia, which was so cheerful, and Belgrade, where you left so many friends. You arrived there in November of 1925. There was a parish priest reading his prayer book in your train compartment. That struck you. You took it as a sign and noted it in your journal. The eastern train station seemed dreary and mysterious to you. All the routes crisscrossed . . .

Would this memory of your arrival come to mind in December of 1943, eighteen years later, when you left from this same station in ominous cars heading for Buchenwald?

For the moment, however, you needed to find the St. Sergius Theological Institute. I imagine you getting off at the Botzaris metro station[1] and walking along the Buttes-Chaumont Park looking for Crimea Street, which you would undoubtedly come to associate with the Black Sea and its subtropical shore. Cruelly disenchanting were the houses black with soot. There was nothing charming about this largely poor working-class Parisian neighborhood. You wrote in your journal:

---

[1]   They say when Metropolitan Eulogius got off at the Botzaris station, he found a resemblance between it and the Slavonic word *votsaris,* the imperative of the verb "to reign." "Reign, Tsar Boris," he said to Mikhail Osorgin, who showed him the land that had been taken and put up for auction in 1924. As for the park Buttes-Chaumont, the metropolitan found that it was an ideal place to meditate and pray, as did crowds of students and parishioners of the St. Sergius Institute.

Strange city—hostile and cold. I didn't imagine that the Saint Sergius metochion would be like this. The notions of time and place are bizarre. It would be strange to go back to Belgrade, if God wills that I return.

The founders of St. Sergius Institute of Orthodox Theology wanted it to be a metochion (dependency) of the famous St. Sergius-Trinity Lavra, soon to be desecrated and renamed Zagorsk by the Bolsheviks. When you landed in Paris, the Institute had just opened its doors. Since all of the academies had been closed in Russia, it was in fact the sole establishment for forming those who could serve the Russian Orthodox Church. And in the middle of Paris at that! What passerby could have imagined that he only had to open the door to 93 Crimea Street to find himself suddenly plunged into a completely different world?

There was a small house at the end of the alley whose façade was decorated with an icon of St. Sergius, with a vigil lamp above it. During that period, it was an ordinary seminary kitchen. You turned left and climbed a few stairs between some chestnut trees to reach the famous "Russian Hill" your friends had told you about. The church dominating the hill surprised you since it still looked like a Reformed church. You learned later that it was built in 1864 for a German Protestant colony, but that, by virtue of clauses in the Treaty of Versailles, it was confiscated and auctioned to the spiritual leader of the Russian Orthodox Church, Metropolitan Eulogius, for the trifling sum of four hundred thousand francs. It took a lot of struggle to collect that amount. Decorating it would take place little by little. The iconostasis was limited to a wooden screen decorated with unmatched icons. It wasn't until later that the painter Dmitri Stelletsky[2] would give it the radiant appearance with which we are familiar today.

But where would you stay? Quite simply, under the church, in one of the two dormitories that could accommodate twenty-four students. The beds almost touched, and the mattresses were stuffed with straw. Suitcases went under the beds, and you could hang your cassocks from a nail fastened to the doors or partition screens. As in other boarding houses of the period, the bathrooms were reduced to the minimum—pipes filled with cold water that ran along iron tubs. There was no electricity, and you had to use a gas-operated system that gave off a weak

2   A Russian painter, Dmitri Stelletsky (1875–1947) succeeded in renewing iconographic art.

light and a smell of sulfur. The classrooms were directly adjacent and also under the church. The furniture was simple and the space so confined that sometimes classes would be held in other nearby places such as Manin Street. There were a few buildings in the courtyard, one a candle factory and another a clinic that doubled as a pharmacy. A few professors and their families lived in the others. During the month of November, the trees were almost bare, and the grayish brick façades of the buildings weren't at all cheerful. It was a place that would take some time to get used to.

Classes began in the spring for the first ten registrants in the preparatory year. To get a head start they had to work all summer so they could be placed in the first year. The new batch of students who arrived underwent several tests. There were twenty-three of you. There was difficulty in that every age and degree of education was included, not to mention social background. There were officers of the White Army, taxi drivers, and former students, not necessarily of theology . . . this entire mix would have to live together. Some of them were already priests or monks, but the upheaval of the Revolution had prevented their education. On the contrary, as in your case, others came with only a school-leaving certificate in their pocket. Some didn't even have that, and it was their poor knowledge of French that first pushed them to an institution that could offer them a formation in Russian, along with other things they enjoyed such as Orthodox chant, services, and the appeal of a life in common with compatriots who had experienced the same struggles and who shared in the same difficulties of integration.

The professors knew they would not have well-educated seminarians from the prestigious Kiev and St. Sergius-Trinity academies, where they had not long ago been teaching. But they consoled themselves with the idea that at least here in Paris they wouldn't be oppressed by the heavy burden of synodal inspections. Their chief hierarch, Metropolitan Eulogius, was a man who had exercised his pastoral responsibility in Kholmsk, on the border with Polish Catholics and the frontier of the Russian Empire—a place where Orthodox and Greek Catholics, at that time called "Uniates," lived in a delicate equilibrium. He was well aware of the realities in the Christian world, of its divisions as well as its common ground. He was under the authority of Patriarch Tikhon, who found himself semi-free in a communist world that was hostile to religion. Thus, due to the fact of this separation, Metropolitan Eulogius had a rather unusual degree of freedom. He would take advantage of it by offering a free hand to the St. Sergius professors, while at the same time he visited frequently and carried out his responsibilities as rector.

Far from wanting to establish a Russian Orthodox ghetto in France, the professors of St. Sergius realized the enormous opportunity furnished to them by Providence in confronting them with the Christian West. Bishop Cassian (Bezobrazov) wrote in 1950:

> We are perfectly aware that theological research should on one hand be completely free while on the other hand deeply rooted in Tradition. We aren't closing our eyes to the vital fact that our encounter had considerably enriched us. Before the first World War, we were very familiar with scientific German literature, most of all Protestant. Throughout the following twenty-five years of our work in Paris, we gained access to an enormous amount of both Protestant and Roman Catholic theological thought, French, English, and American. It is in the confrontation of opinion that truth is found. Faced with new problems and enriched by new knowledge, we are brought to formulate responses which were unknown to our forefathers and which we also wouldn't know if the wars and revolutions hadn't changed the face of the world and disturbed our own perspectives.[3]

3   Bishop Cassian (Bezobrazov), *Twenty-five Years of the Institute* (in Russian), *The St. Sergius Metochion in Paris: Seventy-five Years of Existence,* St. Petersburg, editions Aleteia 1999, p. 84.

# *Seminary Life* &c.

&c. *T*HUS THE ST. SERGIUS INSTITUTE ACCEPTED STUDENTS OF very diverse sorts. A semi-monastic status established by Archbishop Benjamin, who was appointed dean, would unite them and help structure their life. Not only were they required to attend and participate in daily services celebrated in the church according to the monastic rite, but they also had to wear cassocks, which denoted their seminarian status. Meals were eaten in silence while listening to lives of the saints. The choir director, Mikhail Osorgin, whose diligence had permitted the archdiocese to acquire the land and buildings, quickly sought out the best voices. The chorus was so large that it could separate into two antiphonal choirs on both sides of the ambo.[1]

You were most certainly among those who could sing, as you were familiar with religious music. In fact, your father Andrey had directed the church choir in Belgrade. He even offered his tuning fork to me when, at the beginning of the 1950s, we finally met each other in Paris. Later on, Sophie Koulomzin would humorously recount your "misadventures" as choir director in one of the RSCM's camps when faced with some girls who didn't have much of a gift for singing.[2] In order to celebrate the Sunday Liturgy appropriately, you made them practice it

---

1   A space which is most often semicircular and slightly raised, located before the royal doors (the center of the iconostasis) between the sanctuary and the nave.
2   Sophie Koulomzin, *Many Worlds, A Russian Life,* St. Vladimir's Seminary Press, 1980 (in English). A Russian edition appeared in Moscow in the Saint-Tikhon edition in 2000 under the title *Miry za Mirami.*

all night at the beach. Much later, you would sing and direct a choir of prisoners at the Royallieu camp in Compiègne.

The type of chant used at the St. Sergius metochion was without Italian flourishes. Rather, it belonged to the *znamenny* style, which both Archbishop Benjamin and Mikhail Osorgin preferred. There were no recordings, and many of the chants were sung from memory. More rarely, compositions by Alexander Kastalsky[3] or—later on—Nikolai Kedrov[4] were used.

In addition, the students were taught to read the hours, matins canon, and the epistle with its prokeimenon[5] in church. Others learned to serve in the altar, to vest the bishop, play bells, light incense, place candles in the trikyrion and dikyrion,[6] and to clean and decorate the church. There were also more humble tasks, such as working in the candle factory, the kitchen, or the garden. Certain young students installed a volleyball net in the court, and taking off their cassocks, would indulge in the pleasure of sports. Nearby Buttes-Chaumont Park would give pleasure to Metropolitan Eulogius—here and there, on benches, beneath the shade of pine trees, next to the lake, or even in the gazebo atop a hill which opened up to a magnificent view of Paris, St. Sergius students would immerse themselves in their books. Parisians strolling by would peer distrustfully at these bearded monks who hadn't taken off their black klobuks[7] and who were conversing with each other in an unknown language.

Who were your fellow-students in that "year zero" at St. Sergius? I'll bet you quickly spotted those who came from Odessa and those who didn't have the absorbed look of the austere seminarian. Your friends included Spassky, Sokolov, and Alexis (later Bishop Nikon) de Greve. The first, Theodosius, came from happy Ukraine and was a rather joyful fellow. Passionate for liturgical music and specializing in the typikon,[8] he later became the choir director in the Parisian RSCM parish

---

3    Alexander Kastalsky (1856–1926) was a great composer of Russian religious music.

4    Nikolai Kedrov (1871–1940) trained a whole generation of choir directors. He greatly enriched the Church's chant repertory with his compositions.

5    Verse placed before one or several verses taken from the Psalms, to which it serves as a response. In the eucharistic liturgy, it is read or chanted before the New Testament readings.

6    Two- or three-branched candlesticks used during hierarchical liturgies.

7    Monastic hat ornamented with a veil.

8    Collection of rules that fix the order and structure of the liturgical offices.

on Olivier de Serres Street. He often talked to me about you. When I was very young, I could feel the affection he had for my little brother and me. Teasing, he would affectionately call us "Fedia," a name he gave to children whom he particularly liked. In an obituary, published in the 1950 St. Sergius Bulletin, he highlighted your simplicity:

> That quality which had hindered him in his studies considerably helped Fr. Dimitri as a pastor. It went hand in hand with a great vivacious spirit which allowed him, when faced with either tragic or comical events, to get to the essential. Once he found the essential, he would act fearlessly, with determination and courage. His death in prison during the war which snatched him from his family and innumerable friends was the crown on the figure of integrity that was Fr. Dimitri. He knew, from beginning to end, how to preserve this God-given simplicity. None of us was appreciated by our hierarchs as much as he. Metropolitans Eulogius and Anthony and other eminent archbishops in Yugoslavia sensed this pastoral gift in him which we saw blossom under the spiritual direction of Elder Sergi Chetverikov and under the influence of Fr. Sergius Bulgakov.

Your simplicity . . . Already at eighteen years old, you wrote in your journal, which I was flipping through when several flower petals fell out:

> I would like for my wicked heart to become as pure and dispassionate as that of the little girl who just offered me these cornflowers. When I asked her who picked them, she did not reply "me," but "we." Such a little adorable heart.

A few pages later, in careful calligraphy, you quoted the Evangelist Mark (10:15): "Amen, I say unto you, whoever does not become like a little child will not enter the kingdom of heaven."

I can see you and Theodosius participating in amusing activities, teasing professors or alumni with jokes that were familiar in boarding schools all over the world, and seminary humor as well. Not only did you work at deciphering Slavonic, the language of Orthodox liturgical offices, but like Latinist schoolchildren of yesteryear, you amused yourself by making fun of it. I found a text in the family archives composed in kitchen Slavonic, which was doubtless a part of a riddle. The victim of the compilation was one of your friends, Mikhail Sokolov, nicknamed "Chel" (from the French Michel) by everyone, who was in charge of waking the students. The text read that he wasn't the rooster (*petel* in Slavonic) they were expecting and that he "measured his sleep by his elbow room." Falling asleep on his elbows, he woke up whenever his arm got stiff. One could also find a savory description of the Parisian metro—you imagine a monk from the Nitrean desert, from the time of St. Basil, discovering "in a vast and somber grotto a fiery dragon transporting compressed humans in its flanks" to a place of perdition called "Duroc" where, on a certain Mount Parnasse, in a house with the ominous number ten, was found another "satanic" place nicknamed the YMCA! As evidence, just as before in Serbia, Parisians had grown no less reticent when they encountered American friends who supported the St. Sergius Institute . . .

Another of your friends was Nikon de Greve, who later became a bishop in the US and Japan. He stayed in touch with my family for a long time. Along with him, when he became a priest, Father Mikhail Sokolov was later to celebrate your marriage in his Colombelles parish near Caen.

Whenever they came to the house, these old seminarians made up a rather lively group. Those who established families stayed in contact with us for a long time; the Sokolov brothers and Spassky were in their turn active members of the Church, choir directors or counselors at Orthodox summer camps.

Another seminarian in your class, Mikhail Yashvil, certainly must have attracted your attention, as you liked humble people and he was the soul of simplicity. He had a passion for railroad engines and musical instruments and preferred to occupy himself with humble tasks such as lighting the censers. It is to him that the church at the St. Sergius Institute owes its belfry. He would spend hours tuning the modest bells acquired by the parish. He had the faith of a working man and had dedicated his life to the Mother of God. He never crossed the street without first making the sign of the cross and reciting the "Rejoice O Virgin." On the handlebars of his bicycle (repainted blue in honor of the Virgin) he had etched four Russian letters: "P.B.S.N.," for "Holy Mother of God Save Us." It was the destiny of his daughter Anastasia (Tassia) to remain a devotee of St. Sergius, where for a long time she took care of the candle stand and was my friend. When her father passed away in 1950, she received the gift of intercession, and it sufficed to report to her the slightest bit of anguish before she would devote herself to prayer.

The same flock also included the future great theologian Paul Evdokimov,[9] who would play a huge role in the rapprochement between Christians. Mother stayed in touch with him, so I suppose that he also was one of your friends.

But now I must abandon this intimate sphere of informality. From now on you have a degree in theology, and your story broadens into a community. It belongs to everyone and becomes destiny.

9  Born in St. Petersburg, Paul Evdokimov (1901–1970) is one of the Orthodox theologians who is most read by French speakers. Engaged in ecumenical dialogue, author of an abundant body of reference books, he was a true "bridge of ideas" between the Eastern Christian world and the West.

# *Love Is Simple* ঙଓ

ঙଓ *T*O HELP ME RECONSTRUCT THE INTERIOR WORLD OF THE seminarian Dmitri Klepinin, I will make use of his journals. He wrote in them the thoughts of St. John of Kronstadt about love and faith: "Love without speculating: love is simple, love is never unfaithful. Believe and hope without speculating, for faith and hope are simple."

On September 4, 1926, he wrote:

> The cell of our deepening is not a closed cavern in which we shut ourselves and cut ourselves off from the world. Rather, it is a temple with transparent walls built on a hill, from which we can see the surrounding areas better than when outside this temple. The deeper we penetrate the sanctuary of this temple, the further we move away from the world, the more we shed our blindness and our *a priori* concept of the world; when our miserable and conceited intellect humbles itself and becomes the spirit of God. In sacrificing self-love, we acquire that free will of the man who carries out God's will. In fact, whoever carries out this will is free of tormenting questions such as "What is to be done?" or "Pray and fast or serve my fellow man?" He follows the commands of the Holy Spirit Who invisibly touches his conscience.

Three years later, Dmitri returned to this intuition about the invisible action of the Spirit:

> Spiritual progress comes about without man's realizing it. He always remains just as impoverished, but what are the fruits of this? They

undoubtedly reside in that man feels more and more that the Lord is all for him. Christ is my strength . . . You are my rampart, Lord, You are my strength, You are my God, You are my joy. Or, as Saint Paul says: it is not I who live, but Christ who lives in me.

His journal is filled with advice for himself: "You must receive communion more often in order to be with Christ." Or further:

To start the day out well, you need to rise early, and gathering your thoughts, pray to God unhurriedly. Pray for all that awaits you, implore God's help for every affliction that could come throughout the day. When you expect these things, they won't appear as frightening in the moment they appear.

He often returned to prayer:

If during prayer you feel neither sweetness nor warmth, you ought to continue praying without discouragement, knowing that it is just that that will bring about progress. Center your attention on understanding the content of the words and their application to life. Prayer should apply to life, each word resonating with the everyday. To pray attentively means to open your entire life to the Lord, both its faults and its needs. It means asking for help against all the temptations that can arise. This also comes back to reconsidering your entire being and life. It awakens sweetness and warmth. Thus prayer of the mind precisely becomes prayer of the heart.

The theme of the cross is also present in his reflections: "We see a cross on the church bell towers. This cross raised on Golgotha attracts to it all the cardinal points. The Lord said that when He was raised on a tree He would draw the whole world to Himself."

As a conclusion he wrote: "What's important is to remain faithful to the end, to be honest towards yourself."

# The Jesus Prayer ❧

❧ In 1931 reader Dmitri Klepinin presented a Master's thesis entitled, "The Heart and the Mind in the Jesus Prayer." I do not know whether he picked this theme or whether it was assigned to him. However, in approaching it, Dmitri brought together the hesychastic tradition revived by Paisius Velichkovsky,[1] which was very present in Russia, Romania, and Serbia during those troubled times. What were the principal ideas of the 215-page handwritten notebook?

Dmitri began by posing the question: Is it possible to pray ceaselessly as St. Paul commands us to do? Yes, on the condition that we rediscover the interior man, take control of all our thoughts, every movement of the soul and especially of the heart towards our Creator; if we become people of prayer, acquiring "interior lips" that praise the Lord at all times and every hour.

Making a list of the various short prayers used by the Fathers, he emphasized that the power of the prayers resides in their very brevity. They can, in fact, at any moment and under any circumstances return as a leitmotiv, whereas long prayers rouse the spirit and lead it astray. Citing the example of St. Ignatius of Antioch,[2] to whom he was very

---

1   Monk and spiritual father on Mount Athos and then in Moldavia, Paisius Velichkovsky (1722–1794) is notably the translator and editor in Slavonic of the *Philokalia of the Watchful Fathers,* a great classic of Orthodox literature on the ascetic life and prayer.

2   First bishop of Antioch, Ignatius (+ 100–117) was martyred at Rome under the reign of Trajan. He is the author of the Letters, which constitute the fundamental text, after the New Testament, for understanding the vision of the first Christians.

close, Dmitri says that when St. Ignatius, who is called the God-bearer, was given over to torture under the reign of Trajan, he did not cease repeating the name of Jesus inscribed on his heart.

The Jesus Prayer, Dmitri points out, is Christocentric. It constitutes a summary of our salvation by Christ, but at the same time it is aimed at the Father, because Jesus said, "No one shall come to the Father but by Me" (John 14:6). The Jesus Prayer is theology in a nutshell, a summary of our faith. It makes us conscious of the gulf that separates us from divinity, which is why it ends with the cry, "have mercy on me, a sinner."

Our contrition, though, should not be colored with despair because God is present in us. Not only can He free us from our sin, but He can also grant us His grace. If the first part of the Jesus Prayer is contemplative, the second is active, while the two are interactive. It is because we recognize and proclaim that the Lord Jesus Christ is the Son of God that we are able to call on Him to have mercy on us. The goal to reach is the state described by the Apostle when he says, "It is not I who live, but Christ who lives in me."

St. Theophan the Recluse explains that there are three degrees in the Jesus Prayer: oral prayer, mental prayer, and prayer of the heart. The most difficult thing is to cast the mind into the heart. It is solely here that the Lord visits the soul in prayer.

The spiritual father determines the number of repetitions according to his disciple's state of advancement. The disciple must dedicate a certain time of his day to prayer and find adequate space. In fact, one must be aware of everything that may contribute to making us available to speak with God. In the first place, the Eucharist—practice the Jesus Prayer before and after receiving communion. This is an excellent practice for conserving the grace of the Divine Visitor that has entered us. In the second place, we should read the Holy Scripture and the Church Fathers, as well as all those who have transfigured the old man within themselves. When we read the lives of the saints we no longer feel alone. We realize that they were ordinary men who overcame, not by their own power, but by the intervention of God in their lives.

In order to surmount the scattering of his attention, the one praying must make an effort to hold himself upright and regulate his prayers by bending his body, in metanoias or prostrations, unless he feels that these movements disturb his concentration. Even so, the Fathers recommend beginning by saying the words out loud so that in the second stage one may enter more deeply into the prayer and pray in silence. They propose using a prayer rope to count the sequence, but insist on the fact that it is not the number but rather the fervor that constitutes good prayer.

One must not expect to receive any particular grace during this exercise. The only goal to seek is concentration. This is the most difficult because we are ceaselessly being assailed by our thoughts. One defense used to ward them off is pugnacity or directing holy anger towards them. It is a fight with the devil who, as the parable of the seven demons shows, is constantly waiting for the moment to return to the house from which he was driven, if that house is not filled with the Spirit of God. Another defense is the remembrance of death. To think, when going to bed, that God could come even tonight and take back one's life—this helps a man to give himself entirely to God. This is why the true ascetic prays even during sleep.

But how does the mind descend into the heart? The separation between the mind and the heart is the consequence of the Fall. Our inner being takes pleasure in the law of God, whereas our members indulge in a contrary law. We are broken vessels. In order to find the path towards God again, we must capture the mind and turn away from the flesh, participating with Christ in our own salvation.

If Jesus the Son knew how to resist Satan's temptations in the desert, it is because His being had not lost its primary harmony with His Father; He was abiding in the love of God, and in obedience, voluntarily emptied Himself. In Jesus Christ came a new form of relationship between God and humanity. We have been adopted by God and anointed by the Holy Spirit when the Church was born at Pentecost. Equally from this came the importance of our salvation in the Church. It is through the Church that we have access to the sacraments of baptism and the Eucharist, which help us to make use of the talents given to us.

Following the commandments does not give meritorious grace by which man attains eternal life. Rather, the commandments open the door to our soul in order that Christ might live in us here and now, as it is written, "As many as have been baptized into Christ have put on Christ" (Galatians 3:27). Cleansed of original sin by baptism, the human being nonetheless remains a broken vessel, which he spends his whole life reconstructing. "Take My yoke and learn of Me, for I am gentle and humble of heart." This yoke is our way of being crucified with Christ. By taking it we come to know relief, as Jesus adds, "My burden is light" (Matthew 11:28–30). The more man convinces himself of the Savior's sweetness, the more he frees himself from his attachment to the flesh and the life of this world. He becomes like that man in the parable who found the pearl of great price and sold everything in order to own it.

All asceticism comes back to freeing the heart from the desires of the flesh, submitting our will to spiritual principles, and delivering our will to Christ. Here is realized the union of the mind and the heart and their submission to Christ. But by what method do we gain access but by prayer? The Jesus Prayer is particularly propitious in this effort of reuniting the human being with himself. By practicing it, we will see the fruits which St. Paul calls the "fruits of the Spirit"—love, joy, peace, patience, kindness, goodness, faithfulness, humility, and self-control (see Galatians 5:22, 23). In order to acquire the gift of humility it is best to defer to a spiritual father.

If prayer of the heart is a gift from God, it is also a constant labor, which goes along with the struggle against the passions. It demands that one build one's entire life on endeavoring and on the other, by turning towards the next life. For accomplishing the law of love means opening oneself to God.

External methods exist for uniting the mind with the heart. Thus, St. Symeon the New Theologian recommends a certain number of concentration techniques. Particularly important is the frequency of prayer exercises because it establishes a positive schedule.

When we attain an elevated state in the spiritual life, the Jesus Prayer becomes as necessary to us as the air we breathe. It is transformed into a permanent glorification wherever we are and whatever we do, even in the heart of sleep: "I sleep, but my heart is awake" (Psalm 5:2). The Way of the Pilgrim reveals at what point this high degree of praise transfigures man's view of nature. He experiences a permanent sense of wonder as he comes to understand the language of plants and animals, and tears of joy flow from his eyes. Many of the lives of the saints show us the profound union with nature that ascetics can attain. Thus, St. Seraphim of Sarov fed his bear. These saints pity creation and pray even for the fallen angels. These are the fruits of prayer of the heart.

Prayer then is a precious method of communion with the divine, a path leading to salvation.

I don't know whether this very dense but classic thesis has been approved by the professor who posed the question. We owe it to Dmitri's fellow alumnus Theodosius Spassky, who kept it. He found it in a cupboard at the St. Sergius Institute, where he was the librarian. He passed it on to us, adding with a mocking tone, "You might as well be the one who has it—here there is a risk of its disappearing. There are tons of students' notebooks piled up in boxes . . ."

# Nikolai, His Older Brother ⳥

⳥ SIX YEARS ROLLED BY BETWEEN THE PRESENTATION OF THAT
Master's thesis and the time Fr. Dimitri entered the priesthood. We
know practically nothing of that period of his life except that they
were difficult years, as much with respect to his finances as his frame
of mind. He was living in Paris then on rue des Plantes at the home of
his brother Nikolai, who was often gone. He was helping him to mon-
itor the Soviet press. Nikolai, in fact, was looking for examples of the
antireligious campaign that was raging in the USSR to compile arti-
cles he published in a "tri-monthly non-political bulletin based on information contained in the Soviet press." He extracted certain examples that were stupefying in their naiveté. For example, a Soviet teacher
recounted how she succeeded in demonstrating to her students that
God does not exist:

> I suggested that the children prepare two plots to cultivate vegetables.
> We put a lot of effort into one, hoeing it and watering it as farmers do.
> As for the other, we left it as it was. We would see if any God could make
> vegetables grow there. In fact, on June 26, in the first plot, we harvested
> fennel, radishes, and beans. But nothing appeared in the plot that be-
> longed to the good Lord. I asked the children why nothing came up in
> that plot.
> —We didn't cultivate it.
> —But it belongs to the good Lord. Why didn't He take care of it?
> —God doesn't exist. In the sky there is nothing but air and clouds, re-
> plied most of the children.

Suddenly I suggested a song to them:

We didn't hoe or water the plots.
We just turned toward the sky.
We waited for help from God,
But nothing came up, nothing all summer.
In the sky there is nothing but air and clouds,
But there is no god.

What was most amusing was that the children added a refrain:

Down with monks, down with popes!
We'll climb up to the sky and chase away God!

One could find no more striking and convincing illustration that Russian atheism considered itself to be above all a struggle against a God who really does exist. . . .

Nikolai Klepinin was really a very strange personality . . . My mother, who barely knew him, used to say that he was very versatile, capable of denying one day what he had defended the evening before. In fact, his political convictions went through great variations. He had been a volunteer in the White Army, fought communism in the Crimea, and followed General Wrangel into exile. In France he was also an adherent of the "Eurasian" movement, which defended a historical and political concept of a radical opposition between Russia and Europe. According to them, Russia was rooted in the Mongol tradition, being the heir of the great Tatar khans, the continuer of the work of Genghis Khan, and the reunifier of Asia. The Eurasians dreamed of participating in the spiritual renaissance of Soviet Russia. In 1927 Nikolai published a work on St. Alexander Nevsky in which he highlighted the saint's very respectful policy in regard to the khans—a very debatable thesis according to the historian George Fedotov.[1]

The Eurasian movement was, in fact, infiltrated by the communists. Nikolai belonged to the "Union for the Return to the Fatherland" founded in 1924 in Paris with the assistance of the GPU,[2] later

---

1  George Fedotov (1886–1951) was a historian and professor at the St. Sergius Institute.
2  The GPU was the political directorate of the USSR, created in 1923 with the aim of "fighting against the counter-revolution."

the NKVD.[3] He was soon mixed up in a shadowy affair—the assassination of Ignaty Reiss, a Soviet secret agent who had just gone over to the other side. Sought by the French police, Nikolai was hastily repatriated to the USSR with his family in 1937, at the same time as Sergey Efron, the husband of the poetess Marina Tsvetayeva (1892–1941). We can imagine the shock this brutal departure must have produced on Dmitri during that crucial year of his marriage and ordination. The two brothers really were quite different, in fact, but they were deeply attached to one another.

The Klepinin family had no idea of the fate in store for the victims that were ground up by the Soviet machine. It was only in 1961 that we learned that Nikolai and his wife Antonina had been arrested and tortured by the NKVD and then executed by firing squad on July 6, 1941. They had left behind them a daughter, Sophia, who became not only a specialist in the work of Tsvetayeva but also the guide to the dacha which had been turned into a little museum at Bolshevo. In particular she would tell visitors how her parents had lived the last years of their life in that very special house, which was monitored by the secret police. The last image the witnesses had of Nikolai was that of a man being hunted down, gripping his bulldog closely to him, and picked up by the police one windy day of November 1939.

After questioning those who were close to Nikolai and those who were interested in the Eurasian movement, I understood that he lived through his return to the USSR as a sort of mission—without illusions about the totalitarian system, he formed the naïve hope that if he could not reform it then at least he could ameliorate it. But that was because he did not take into account the perversity of the totalitarian machine. That machine recruited agents, but once it had no more need of them, it considered them to be troublesome witnesses and ended up liquidating them unscrupulously on grounds which were often completely fallacious. The file of charges against the Klepinin couple, to which their daughter had access after *perestroika*, contains in fact some of the most fantastic accusations. We also know that they were tortured.

3   The NKVD was the People's Commissariat for Internal Affairs. Created in 1917, suppressed in 1930, it was reestablished in 1934 and absorbed the GPU. Police surveillance of individuals, camps, deportation, and work details belonged to the NKVD, which extended its branches outside of Russia, keeping the activities of Russian émigré organizations under surveillance and infiltrating them with agents.

# *Amorous Feelings* ଚଙ

ଚଙ THE INTERVAL BETWEEN THE END OF HIS THEOLOGICAL studies and his entry into the priesthood was a sad period for Dmitri. He wandered a little, searched for himself, not really knowing how to orient his life. In particular he stayed for a while in Czechoslovakia, where he met Fr. Sergius Chetverikov,[1] who would later have a great influence on him. He served as his chanter in Bratislava. They would meet again later in Paris and in the RSCM youth camps.

After he returned to Paris, Dmitri undertook various jobs to provide for his needs. He waxed floors and washed windows right and left. He felt lonely and useless. He wanted to become a priest but he didn't have a vocation for monasticism. He had to get married, then. But how could he find a kindred spirit? Metropolitan Eulogius used to say humorously that the Orthodox circles of Paris decided to marry off Dmitri.

For two years Dmitri hoped that Sophia Shidlovskaya, in whom he was interested, would respond to his love. It was hard, in fact, to resist the charms of that young lady with the round cheeks and the glance full of life and intelligence. Sophia was born in 1903 in Russia. She had kept a warm memory of the charms of patriarchal life on her parents' property. She had known revolution, despoliation, and exile, but she retained her optimism and energy throughout every trial. She very

---

1 Ordained a priest in Russia in 1896, graduate of the Theological Academy of Moscow, Fr. Sergius Chetverikov (1867–1947) emigrated to Yugoslavia, then to Czechoslovakia, where he was rector of the Russian parish of Bratislava from 1923 to 1928. In Paris he was the spiritual father of RSCM.

quickly put herself in contact with the Americans of the YMCA who worked in Russia, Estonia, and then in France. Seeing Sophia's abilities as an educator, the YMCA obtained a grant for her from the Rockefeller Foundation to study work methods for catechizing children. In this way she spent a year in New York and came back to Paris full of enthusiasm to work in the midst of the RSCM. That is where Dmitri made her acquaintance in 1927. They were the same age, both members of RSCM, and they often saw one another at the movement headquarters on boulevard Montparnasse. Sophia organized youth camps, and Dmitri was invited as an assistant cook or chanter. In the collection of memoirs she published at the end of her life,[2] Sophia wrote some bold things about the bashful young man who courted her:

> Dima Klepinin played a great role in my life. Our connection dates from the summer camps when he directed the youth choir. It seems to me that he had in him that quality we call holiness. Dima, who was physically rather unattractive, very near-sighted, and short, was loveable and good-spirited. He was very straightforward and radiated wisdom and love. In contact with him one felt a weight lifted, and everything became simple and easy to understand. When he spoke with you it was as if a ray of light shone over your life. We took different paths and I married . . .

Several years ago, Sophia, who lived in the United States with her family, entrusted to me the letters that Dmitri sent her in 1929 and 1930. It is a moving correspondence, full of delicacy and tenderness. In August 1930, when Sophia was directing the vacation camp for the girls of the RSCM, Dmitri, who stayed in Paris, suggested to her that they always pray at the same hour. "This," he wrote, "will be our form of communion." They each had a favorite star, and it consoled him to gaze at them at night. On his table he put a photograph of the camp in order, as he explained, to better imagine the life of the dynamic young lady. Very tactfully he raised the subject of their future and left Sophia at complete liberty: "Have no fear, if you decide not to unite your life with mine, I will see a manifestation of the divine will and we will go together to the church to celebrate a moleben."[3]

2  Sophie Koulomzin, op. cit.
3  A *moleben* in the Russian tradition is a prayer service asking for God's grace.

Dmitri offered Sophia his reflections on God's will:

The Lord required that Abraham offer Him—to Him, his God—his only
son Isaac as a sacrifice. How cruel that seems! Now, He required Isaac in
order to give him back, and through Isaac, to assure him of a posterity
more numerous than the grains of sand by the sea. The same happened
with Job. The lives of unbelievers seem happy, while God seems to deny
the prayers of believers who supplicate Him to assure their prosperity.
Why does that happen? We must see in it a proof of God's love. Unbelievers, in fact, do not expect anything from God, and so God does not
take anything from them. They perceive everything they receive as coming from themselves, and they do not see in it any supernatural gift or
any divine intervention.

Each of us has a destiny here below which was traced out from the
beginning of the world. This destiny takes the form of a potential. We
do not escape it if we do not oppose God's plan. Who we are and where
we are is not a matter of indifference to God. Each person is precious in
His eyes. And so if He guides us and we do not recognize that it is He
Who directs us, we will not know happiness.

In the month of September 1930, Dmitri participated in the RSCM
congress at Monfort l'Amaury, during which he was assigned to prepare the church for the morning liturgies. He wrote Sophia a letter full
of mature thought on the nature of love in the New Testament. Sophia
found these reflections so profound that she recopied them and kept
them as something precious. On Fr. Dimitri's death these thoughts
were reproduced and sent to his loved ones. They were published in the
issue of *Vestnik*[4] dedicated to the priest-martyr.

Remember: St. Paul said that love is the basis of the law. The Old Testament does not offer a practical explanation of this love in the law. It
simply establishes just relations between men and between men and
God. Such also is love in modern humanism—it is a means or a force
that organizes and transforms life. In both cases, this comes from the
fact that men are incapable of making enough space within themselves
for this love. But in fact God's attitude toward men is always the same
because God does not change.

4   *Vestnik,* No. 168, II–III 1993. In Russian.

In the New Testament, by contrast, the utilitarian sense of love disappears. The commandments are similar about the tunic someone demands and the coat they do not demand, the mile someone asks you to go and the second mile they do not ask you to go. In this case, he who gives forgets the reason for his gift and concentrates on the person who asks. Then the barrier fades between oneself and the other person. The summit is surely attained with the washing of the disciples' feet and the passion on the cross.

Such also is the parable of the prodigal son. The Old Testament is limited to the son's desire to return to his father's house as a day-laborer, while God shows the fullness of His relationship with man by clothing him with a rich tunic, putting a ring on his finger, and slaying the fatted calf for him.

It is significant that in the life of the age to come there is neither faith nor hope. Nothing will remain but love which has been freed of all utilitarianism. This love is undeniably the very content of life, for life was created by love—God is love—and it consists in returning to its primary foundation: love. Everything else is a testing of the will to see whether it will move in this sense, and bring about this return. Everything positive increases beginning with love, and everything negative— the false expression of love—is a parasite on the body of love.

Such, then, is the origin of all sin, whose consequence is suffering— estrangement from love. My way of considering sin is perhaps heretical, but I find there is something worse than sin—a utilitarian love, a love for God and men without a love story. It is frightening because the purpose of life is to return to the source of love, which is Christ. Sin can emerge in the consciousness of the void, while utilitarian love is a heresy which makes life an end in itself and turns love into harmony. In reality life is destined to put love to the test. In the life of the age to come, life will be love and love will be life.

The relationship between Dmitri and Sophia stopped there. Another man entered her life—Nikita Koulomzin. Dmitri stepped aside and went to Serbia, and from there he sent her a last letter of farewell. He was profoundly defeated.

Full of emotion, I was reading Dmitri's letters to Sophia, when one of them seemed to wink at me complicitly: "I spent Sunday at the house of Tamara Fyodorovna Baimakova. She had invited some friends when a girlfriend of hers arrived from Prague and she prepared an excellent *cruchon*." This detail made me smile. *Cruchon*, a sort of sangria with white wine, is in fact a family recipe. It served as a love potion between my parents.

# ❧ V ❧

# *Entry into the Priesthood*

# Tamara, His Future Spouse ❧

❧ WRITTEN IN A NOTEBOOK IN 1954 IN A BEAUTIFUL REGU-
lar hand, the lines that follow describe my mother. That year, she had
to take part in an ecumenical congress during which the participants
had to introduce themselves, and she put down in French the stages of
her life which she judged to be essential, a kind of autobiography. She
was fifty-seven years old and had been a widow for ten years:

I was born near Saint Petersburg and am a member of the Orthodox
Church. I left Russia in 1921, and I worked for seven years as the secretary for the Russian section of the YMCA in Riga (Latvia). I took part in
several international YMCA conferences (St. Wolfgang, Saint-Cergue,
Sonntagsberg) as well as in the local Baltic conferences. I was sent in
1924 to Selly Oak in England to study for a trimester at the College of
the Ascension.

Through my work in Riga I had numerous contacts with Protestants.
The conferences have held great importance for the ecumenical movement, since we always had Protestant, Orthodox and even sometimes
some Roman Catholic delegates.

In the meantime, Paris became the intellectual and spiritual center of the Russian émigré elite. After meeting the most brilliant professors such as Berdyaev, Zenkovsky, Frank,[1] Vysheslavtsev,[2] and Zander,

---

1  Simon Frank (1877–1954), Russian philosopher.
2  Boris Vysheslavtsev (1877–1954), Russian philosopher.

I helped organize their conference tour throughout the Baltic states. This resulted in the creation of the Russian Student Christian Movement (RSCM) in Latvia and Estonia.

In 1929, I left for Paris where I worked with the Russian branch of the American YMCA. I took an active part in the RSCM as well as in ecumenical conferences, in particular in the encounters with French Protestants from the circle of Suzanne de Dietrich[3] and the Anglo-Russian Fellowship of Saint Alban and Saint Sergius.[4] These contacts, and above all those with the Anglicans who were very close to the Orthodox Church, allowed me to deepen my knowledge of my own Church and to realize the universality of the Church and of the eternal values which enable us to understand one another, without however losing any of the riches of our Mother Church.

In 1937, I married a future Orthodox priest, Fr. Dimitri Klepinin, a graduate of the Saint Sergius Theological Institute in Paris and likewise a member of the RSCM and the Fellowship of Saint Alban and Saint Sergius. When the war broke out in 1939, he became the rector of a church founded by a remarkable Russian nun, Mother Maria (Skobtsova), who carried out amazing social work with the destitute, the homeless, the ill, and who organized soup kitchens and workshops.

I helped as best I could and for several months I was the director of a home near Paris whose director had been arrested in 1941. During the Nazi Occupation, Mother Maria and my husband toiled greatly to aid those who were being persecuted by the Gestapo. They were arrested and deported in 1943 and died in 1944.

Since 1945 I have been working again at the YMCA Press, mostly on the publication of the works of Nikolai Berdyaev. Unfortunately, with both family and professional life going on, I don't have a lot of time to dedicate to parish work and the RSCM, even though I participate in its congresses. My two children are members of the Youth section; my sixteen-year-old daughter is a counselor at its summer camps. Her first

3  A Protestant theologian, Suzanne de Dietrich, along with Paul Evdokimov, played an important role in ecumenical rapprochement. In particular, she directed the Center for Theological Research of the World Council of Churches at Bossey (Switzerland).
4  The Fellowship of St. Alban and St. Sergius was founded by a group of Anglican and Orthodox Christians in 1928. Its president was Walter Frier; its vice president was Fr. Sergius Bulgakov. Its purpose was the search for points of convergence between the Anglican and Orthodox confessions.

contact with the Protestant world was a stay at the summer camp at Othona in England.

I would be happy if I succeeded in transmitting to my children the torch of mutual understanding between Christians of all confessions, which has enriched my life so much.

Dear Mother! I recognize her well in this self-portrait. She took such pride in having worked for the Church, for the RSCM and the YMCA, for the great Christian philosophers of the "Paris School"—especially her dear Nikolai Berdyaev—and of having been the faithful companion of Fr. Dimitri. She remained discreet about him and that's normal—she never would elaborate on her private life before an audience that, while certainly well-meaning, was nonetheless unfamiliar. That was her own secret garden, made out of seven years of happiness, seven short years during which she accepted so many sacrifices.

To be the wife of a priest—*matushka* as they say in Russian, *presvytera* in Greek—means in fact agreeing to share all the worries of a clergyman, managing his schedule, responding to requests for meetings with the faithful, being attentive to what's going on in the "side wings" of the parish, helping him morally in bearing the stress of the life of a pastor to a numerous flock. Fr. Dimitri went around a lot in all of Paris and its suburbs for burials, baptisms, weddings, and confessions. Often he would come home late on account of parochial, diocesan, and cultural meetings, solemn services at the cathedral at which the parish rectors' attendance was required. He would often return exhausted, since he had visited the sick, consoled those who were in mourning, calmed the agitated, turned away the suicidal from their noose, admonished the drunken. All this at Lourmel . . . all this during the war and in occupied Paris . . .

I also notice what my mother says of Mother Maria: "Remarkable Russian nun," "amazing social work." She also accepted all this: the home where twenty families were staying, where a hundred people were fed, the lack of privacy, the want of comfort. There were three of us to a room at Lourmel, then four in an attic room under the roof. We had to carry water, coal, and wood up to the fourth floor.

In facing up to all her tasks and responsibilities, Mother in fact had to give up a very interesting job. As the secretary at the YMCA, she accomplished an important task thanks to her good way with people, her organizational skills, and her linguistic knowledge. Her American friends from the RSCM—Donald Lowrie, John Mott, and Paul Anderson—could count on her to reserve a hotel for them on avenue Montaigne, to organize important meetings for them, and to translate their mail. But above all, she knew how to "defend causes," that is, to explain to American benefactors which Christian thinker to publish, which religious association to finance, which Orthodox seminarian to provide with a scholarship.

# The Wedding ✎

✎ The RSCM was a pool not only for priestly vocations, but also for a good number of marriages. In a sense, my parents were an RSCM couple. They announced their engagement at the spring congress of 1937 at Boissy l'Aillerie in the Vexin region. Leon Zander was quick to photograph them sitting on a stump. Mother is radiant, Papa a little confused. I can very well imagine the congratulations and the prayers for "many years."

They chose to go to Colombelles in Normandy for the wedding, to the parish of an eminent alumnus of St. Sergius, Father Mikhail Sokolov—the famous "Chel"—who blessed their union. They were so destitute that they had to borrow a suit from Paul Anderson and had to split in two the gold wedding ring that Tamara got from her mother. The celebration took place on July 12, 1937, the Feast of Saints Peter and Paul, which had always been very dear to Dmitri, who studied their epistles during a semester at the Episcopalian seminary of New York. As Mother told me one day, very moved, a pair of turtledoves came and cooed on the skylight of the church during the Service of Crowning.[1] The newlyweds then left on their honeymoon for several days to the Savoy.

On September 5, Metropolitan Eulogius ordained Dmitri to the diaconate at St. Alexander Nevsky Cathedral in Paris. His ordination to the priesthood took place a week later on September 12, the parish

1  The second part of the Orthodox wedding service, after the Service of Betrothal.

feast. He was then known as Fr. Dimitri, using the Slavonic version of his name.

Were my parents a well-matched couple in the beginning? A friend of my father—a former seminarian like him who only knew my mother slightly—told me of his skepticism once he learned that his "Dimka" had been betrothed to Tamara Baimakova, a woman seven years his senior and (in his eyes) too respectable to be really approachable. Dmitri himself was in anguish. He was just emerging from his disappointing and painful experience of love with Sophia. One night he went to confide his doubts to his friends Natalia and Arkady Terentyev: "Tamara is so much more intelligent, more cultivated than I!" But Natalia, like her sister Valentina Zander, had known Tamara from back in Riga; she reassured Dmitri, who left comforted.

This same friend from seminary also told me to what extent he had changed his mind about Mother, emphasizing that her new role as matushka had made her more sociable, more simple. One of Tamara's friends would later tell me, "Your mother developed a lot in her contact with your father, becoming more approachable and warm."

# *A Very Busy Schedule* ཚ

ཚ D<small>MITRI'S VOW WAS THEN REALIZED AND</small> T<small>AMARA WAS HIS</small> matushka for seven years. "I helped as best I could," she wrote, very modestly. Metropolitan Eulogius appointed Fr. Dimitri as the second priest of the parish of the Presentation of the Virgin in the Temple at 91 rue Olivier de Serres, in the Fifteenth Arrondissement where many Russians lived. A small leather datebook, providentially found in the bottom of my cellar, provides me with a thousand touching details of my father's first steps in his new job as a priest.

For the first year of his priesthood, 1937–1938, the pages of the calendar are filled by the priest and his matushka. It is their family and parish datebook, indispensable, in which they noted everything that thenceforth made up their daily life as a couple in service of the Church. Mother took her role very seriously; she wrote in the dates of the Lenten Triodion[1] for her husband, the birthdays and feast days. He himself put in everything related to his ecclesiastical service.

Taking first place are the liturgies at his parish, where he and Fr. Lev Liperovsky took turns celebrating. The parish rector in name was Fr. Sergius Chetverikov, who however was in retirement at the monastery of Valamo in Finland. He wrote to his parishioners that he was happy to be replaced by two priests who had experience with Christian youth and who had participated so closely in the creation of the RSCM. Later, when the metropolitan attached Fr. Dimitri to Lourmel,

---

[1]   The liturgical service book of Great Lent, which precedes Pascha (Easter).

he was sorry that the parish had not found the financial means to ensure a sufficient salary to Fr. Dimitri and his family so as to keep them at Olivier de Serres.[2] The word "Lourmel" appears for the first time in the datebook in the middle of the year.[3] Since the meetings took place in the evening, one can assume this refers to the talks organized by Mother Maria or to Vespers.

Numerous baptisms also figure in the datebook. The young priest just starting out notes that he must not forget to ask the complete name and religion of the godparents, which he would enter in the parish registers. He was still unaware that these famous entries in what the Russians call "the metrics book," the parish register, would punctuate his way of the cross under the German Occupation.

Finally there are funerals in great number. Certainly the Russians were numerous in Paris, but one is still struck by the number of days on which the calendar abounds with notations of this kind: "Aisle 6, division 8, tomb 42." The sick are no less in number: "Salpetrière Hospital, service of Prof. So-and-so, bed 14." As a matter of fact, the diocese delegated a hospital section to each priest. For Fr. Dimitri, these were the Boucicault and Laënnec hospitals, but I assume that if a parishioner or friend had been hospitalized elsewhere, he would go there as well.

The metropolitan also sent him to celebrate in the suburbs in the parishes of Rosay-en-Brie and Ozoir-la-Ferrière; Fr. Dimitri copied down the train or bus schedules. One day he went as far as Nevers: "Aisle 16, division 4."

We have an account of the burial, by Fr. Dimitri, of the poet Konstantin Balmont[4] at Noisy-le-Grand on December 23, 1942:

> "I have come into this world to see the sun." With these words he began his homily that was so simple, so full of radiant truth, as he himself was, our priest so humble and gentle, the irreplaceable Fr. Dimitri Klepinin who immediately felt the spirit of the poet and of the small group of people who had come to bid him farewell.[5]

2   This handwritten letter of Fr. Sergius was given to me by Fr. Igor Vernik, who revered my father.
3   In Paris, parishes are often referred to by the name of the street on which the church is located.
4   Konstantin Balmont (1867–1942), Russian poet.
5   Account of M. N. Yakimova, quoted by P. Kuprianov in *La Pensée russe* (Paris).

Fr. Dimitri took advantage of his trips by train to review the funeral service, since the list of *ecphoneses*[6] in his notebook starts with "Holy God"[7] and concludes with "Memory eternal."[8] Or perhaps he read some book and copied quotations or prayers.

Prof. Basil Zenkovsky, the parish warden, noted that his former student celebrated with a lot of concentration. The presence of numerous servers in the sanctuary and their incessant coming and going would irritate him; he asked the warden not to bring him the prosphora[9] and the diptychs[10] of offering all the time, but only at the proskomedia and just before the Cherubic Hymn so that he could be entirely present to what he did when serving. The parishioners could feel the atmosphere of prayer and mystical tension that streamed forth through the royal doors.

On Tuesday, May 10, 1938, my parents had to go together to a meeting. A surprising exchange figures in the datebook. Mother writes: "The ineffectiveness of the League of Nations derives from the fact that it is without any metaphysical foundation." Papa's handwriting responds: "For as the heavens are higher than the earth, so are my ways higher than your ways and my thoughts higher than your thoughts." A touching dialogue: Mother was always interested in ideological debates, and Papa replied to her through the mouth of the Prophet Isaiah! In this year in which the Munich Accords[11] were signed, the name of Hitler appears more and more often. I know from Mother's accounts that the Fuhrer's racist theories were fiercely denounced in the circles my parents frequented. Moreover, they decided themselves to study the question more closely and bought an edition of *Mein Kampf* in German.

In addition, they would attend on some Tuesdays the meetings of the Brotherhood of the Holy Trinity[12] initiated by Fr. Sergius Bulgakov. These meetings often took place in the apartment of Leon and

6  The doxological conclusion of a prayer or litany, chanted by the celebrant.
7  "Holy God, Holy Mighty, Holy Immortal, have mercy on us."
8  Final chant in a memorial service.
9  Offertory loaves.
10 List of the living and the dead who are commemorated during the preparation of the Holy Gifts of the Eucharist.
11 Shameful accords passed in 1938 between France, Great Britain, and Hitler, which permitted the annexation of Czechoslovakia by Germany and unleashed World War II.
12 Brotherhood formed by the friends and spiritual children of Fr. Sergius Bulgakov. Its members engaged in prayers for one another and met for spiritual discussions.

Valentina Zander. Who took part? One can find out from a photograph dating from the years 1940–1941, taken by Leon Zander, who loved to be defined as a philosopher and photographer. All the members of the Brotherhood surround their bishop at the cathedral on rue Daru. Valentina Zander has her beautiful face with sad eyes; her little daughter Maria, a child with Down's Syndrome, is proud to pose at the feet of Metropolitan Eulogius. They are all there, my parents' close friends who would later become mine: the iconographer Tamara Elchaninova—the widow of Fr. Alexander[13]—and her children, Maria and the very young Kirill, who would play so large a role in my life as the head of the RSCM's youth section, in which I would make my start as a counselor. Fr. Boris Stark[14] and his wife are there, who after the war would return to the USSR to Yaroslavl and whom I would visit in 1980. Fr. Boris told me that Fr. Dimitri knew the order of services much better than he: "You know, he had studied at St. Sergius and celebrated every day at Lourmel, whereas for me, I would celebrate mainly on feast days. Once during a congress, we were preparing daily Vespers with difficulty, and he being mischievous teased us: 'You're nothing but Sunday priests!'"

Natalia and Arkady Terentyev are also members of the group, pillars of the parish at rue Olivier de Serres; the archpriest Alexander Chekan, his wife and their son Ivan,[15] seated in the first row, as well as the Karpushkos: Pyotr, Elena—who would have a tragic death—and the young Sasha, crouched down at the feet of Fr. Dimitri, who apparently is tickling his back, since the little boy is laughing wildly. This reminds me of another photo taken in 1938 in the courtyard at Olivier de Serres, in which Fr. Dimitri is embracing one of the Spassky boys. One senses that he had a particular affection for these children; on this topic I have an account directly from my friend Sasha Karpushko, who was sent by his mother at the age of eight to confess to Fr. Dimitri after running away. I cite his letter from 1996:

13  Fr. Alexander Elchaninov (1881–1934), Orthodox priest and author of spiritual works. In English: *Diary of a Russian Priest,* SVS Press, 1982.

14  Fr. Boris Stark (1906–1996) was for a long time in charge of the Orthodox cemetery of Sainte-Geneviève-des-Bois, near Paris. He had compiled an impressive list of the names of deceased parishioners for whom he prayed.

15  Ivan Chekan (born in 1933) is one of the founders of the Orthodox Press Service and one of the moderators of the Ecumenical Encounters at Pomeyrol in the Vaucluse.

Your father received me at confession with joy. I have a text about Mother Maria in which he is described during the Paschal feast as radiant with light. That's how he received me, without the slightest reproach, happy that I exist. This was a problem for me: how can batiushka be happy to see us who are so dirty and who come precisely to lay plain our impurities? I understood this much later. The contact with the holiness on Mount Athos proved to me that such men are filled with wonder not by the short-lived, sinful, erring being and "prodigal son" that we are, but by the aptitude each one has for holiness. They see the saint we are able to be: each one different, incomparable, marvelous.

The young priest's skill at listening must have become known, and the Russians of the Fifteenth Arrondissement came in droves to be confessed. One of the parishioners relates how Fr. Dimitri confessed them:

He had a Socratic kind of mind and would respond to the most difficult questions in the simplest way, often by another question. One day, I am confessing to him my distraction during the services. I can't help noticing the faces, the postures, even the color of the clothes of the faithful. He reflects and says: "How can we do otherwise?" Another time, very frustrated, I reproached him for his exceeding leniency. Well, he gave me a light thump on the shoulder and said to me: "Because you imagine to yourself that I am without sins?" [16]

Theodore Pianov [17] does not hesitate to say that confessing to Fr. Dimitri was a real spiritual event. Sometimes, when the priest felt that the penitent was having difficulty in freeing his conscience, he would take the first steps and would confess himself, which invariably would release the tension and allow the reticence and resistance to be overcome. This confessional pedagogy goes back to an old tradition attested by the practice of the Desert Fathers.

---

16 Account of Maria Kravchenko. H.K.A. archives.
17 Theodore Pianov (1889–1969) was the faithful companion of Mother Maria (Skobtsova), the secretary of Orthodox Action, and the director of the retirement home in Noisy-le-Grand. Rescued from the camp of Buchenwald, he participated in the commemoration services dedicated to Fr. Dimitri and Mother Maria.

# *Priest & Father*  ∽

∽ *I*N THIS SAME YEAR OF 1938, MOTHER WAS ALSO EXPECT-
ing her first child. Fr. Dimitri writes in the notebook the telephone
number of the clinic and a list of errands: "crystallized sugar, milk,
rolled oats." On June 10, Mother notes: "Helen is born." Papa must have
been overcome by the events, since his handwriting is a jumble: "Eau de
cologne, two terry towels, small pillowcase, Dumesnil beer" . . . With
these very eloquent details, I think about that particular June—the visits to the clinic where one of the midwives is Russian, the congratulations of the parishioners and friends who had prayed so much that
this child be born, the pastoral marathon of baptisms, burials, visita-
tions, celebrations . . .

"Wedding of George and Kira." This simple mention on Saturday,
July 30, brings me back to our family—Kira is Mother's niece, the only
daughter of her sister Nina. She was beautiful, all blonde, and her cas-
cading laugh was infectious. She would tell me later:

> It was a very simple wedding at Olivier de Serres. I was living with all of
> you at rue Jouvenet, and your mother left me to deal with the hem of my
> wedding gown all by myself since she had to drop you off at a friend's
> house. My fiancé arrived and seeing me all disconcerted, took the nee-
> dle and finished the hem. After that we went to the church where your
> father was waiting for us!

This story reminds me of another wedding celebrated by Papa at Olivier de Serres—two young people who wanted to get married without the consent of one set of parents came to see him. Something which reminded him of his own difficulties in finding a spouse must have touched him, since he agreed to marry the betrothed couple, afterwards weathering the wrath of the parent who had been defied.

Another time, the situation was even more dramatic—a suicide. The distraught family came to see the priest—would he agree to celebrate a funeral contrary to the canons? Fr. Dimitri agreed, for he understood that this act of desperation was due to a sickness of the soul, and that this man needed the prayers of the Church even more than any other departed soul. The news of it spread and he was lectured by the Church hierarch—he ought to have asked for a dispensation. He explained himself to his metropolitan, who accorded him one.

An entry in the notebook reveals a theme dear to the preacher and confessor—Jesus is at our side here and now. He notes: "The Redeemer is alive in our midst; He Who said, 'I am with you unto the end of the ages,' will ask us if we often sought to meet Him. What will we tell Him?"

The question was more necessary than ever, as World War II broke out some months later. On September 2, 1939, France decreed the general mobilization of armed forces; the following day it declared war on Germany. Male foreigners living in France—stateless or not—had to come before the draft board; they were summoned in alphabetical order. Thus the friends George Kazachkin and Fr. Dimitri Klepinin found themselves in the same barracks, naked as the day they were born, about to line up in front of an officer who would declare them "fit for service." Meanwhile, at the start of the conflict, the "hidden enemy" syndrome was touched off, and France had its first purge of "undesirable" foreigners, who found themselves under lock and key. Among them figured Russian émigrés.

At the home of Orthodox Action—an organization serving the poor and located at 77 rue de Lourmel—Mother Maria (Skobtsova) organized an important meeting on September 24. Its title, "In the Face of New Trials," says a lot about the mindset that animated the group members. They saw it fitting to think of the war as a "sign," an irruption of the wind of history *sub specie æternitatis*. The philosopher

Nikolai Berdyaev would go further in the same vein with a paper on "War and Eschatology"[1] on November 5.[2]

---

1 The English text of this paper may be found at http://www.berdyaev.com/berdi-aev/berd_lib/1939_452.html
2 Nikolai Berdyaev played a great role in the life of my parents. My mother was the editor of a great many of his works and the author of two authoritative bibliographies. My parents attended the Christian thinker's lectures. I have a short note of Berdyaev's to Fr. Dimitri: "I thank you for your words of encouragement; I am all the more sensitive to them, since I am used to being misunderstood." Berdyaev's call to favor the spirit of liberty connected with my parents' deepest convictions.

# *Mother Maria* ❧

❧ THE PARISH OF THE HOME ON RUE DE LOURMEL, CONSE-
crated to the Protection of the Mother of God, was precisely where destiny—or rather, Providence—called my father as rector at the beginning of World War II. It was an extraordinary place founded by Mother
Maria, who would be at the heart of simultaneously heroic and tragic
events linked to the Occupation.

It is difficult to sketch out in a few lines the biography and personality of a figure as rich and complex as that of Mother Maria. The pub-
lisher Maxime Egger sums it up in a book dedicated to her:

> Her life is a novel—epic, tragic, stimulating. Star of the literary salons
> of Saint Petersburg, a revolutionary socialist charged with the task of
> assassinating Trotsky, the mayoress of a small town on the shore of the
> Black Sea, in exile in Europe, the mother of three children—she experi-
> enced everything in her life. Tempted by atheism, she was visited by God
> on the death of her daughter Anastasia. Twice married and divorced,
> she took the monastic habit in 1932 in Paris. But she preferred the des-
> ert of human hearts to the desert of the cloister, the bohemia of a life
> given over to the unpredictable breath of the Spirit to the discipline of
> the convent. Her aim? To conquer the excess of evil by an excess of good.
> Her rule? To give herself completely, to live out her compassion as far
> as the folly of the Cross. In Paris, in the homes which she opened, she

would be the mother of all of life's wounded, the bums, the mentally ill and persecuted Jews.[1]

A theologian and artist, the symbol of her faith and her struggles came forth in the icons she painted, the superb embroideries and designs she produced, and the impassioned texts she wrote on different topics, particularly on the mystical foundations of the relationship with others, the spirituality of social action, the meaning of work, monasticism in the world, the forms of piety and the ascetical life, and the mystery of war.

I imagine that Mother Maria's out-of-the-ordinary personality, her way of life and mode of action gave many people pause. As she herself would say, "for ecclesiastics, we are too far to the left; for leftist groups, too ecclesiastical." One of her main opponents was Archimandrite Kyprian Kern, professor at the St. Sergius Institute, whom Metropolitan Eulogius chose to be priest for the home at rue de Lourmel in the hope that he would be able to lead Mother Maria to the proper path of traditional monasticism. That didn't happen at all. The hieromonk's cold rigorism irritated the nun and awoke her rebellious spirit. Too different in spirit, they had to part ways, and the post was vacant once again.

So it was—and moreover not without apprehension—that the metropolitan appointed Fr. Dimitri as rector of this difficult parish. He took up his functions on October 10, 1939, five days before the parish's patronal feast. A photograph taken by Yuri Skobtsov, Mother Maria's son, immortalizes this event—the day looks to be sunny; Yuri stands with his back to the church and invites the group to the terrace that extends from the house. There's his grandmother, Sophia Pilenko, née de Launay, whom everyone affectionately calls "Babushka" and who is radiant underneath her elegant little black hat. Next to her is Mother Maria in her monastic garb for the days when services are held; her wide face framed by the black cloth of her monastic headdress, she smiles, full of maternal pride.

The new rector visibly does not yet venture to join this family group closely; he stands slightly off to the side, and since he doesn't like to be photographed, is twisting his hands. However, he smiles at Yuri's youth and enthusiasm; he looks in the direction of this modest church

[1]  *Mother Maria,* op. cit.

where he is called to serve. The friends from Orthodox Action also appear in the photo: the historian George Fedotov and the literary critic Konstantin Mochulsky, with whom Yuri loved to travel and visit the cathedrals of France. Alexis Babadzhan—who loved to read in church, since his strong stuttering would then miraculously disappear—is also there, along with a tall, beautiful unidentified lady, who must have taken the second photo so that Yuri could be pictured among those who would come to know great tribulation four years later.

From that moment on, Fr. Dimitri was the full-fledged rector of an important parish. He felt the burden of this new responsibility weigh down on him; this is why his first impulse on that tenth of October in 1939 was to confide in his spiritual father, Fr. Sergius Bulgakov. We have the letter he addressed to him:

Dear Fr. Sergius,

Yesterday I took up my functions as the rector at rue de Lourmel. I would love to talk with you about this new stage of my life and to ask your prayers. I felt abruptly that my own spiritual life was far below what our new situation demanded, whence my feeling very unprepared for the responsibility that the role of pastor entails in this difficult time. Pray for me! If you can, write to me and share your spiritual experience with me. I have a terrible need of being guided constantly and aided daily. These are unprecedented days. However, there are many illuminations: the hand of God can be seen guiding us and producing fruits. This deadly quagmire that is prosperity is about to diminish in the world. Today you can feel the pressing need to pray for the world. One feels that the spiritual world has grown closer to the destinies of peoples; a kind of door has opened to a relationship of prayer with this portion of people who until now have been covered in a layer of grease. But could this be just a figment of my imagination? Do you yourself not feel something approaching? Thus I feel the need to pray to St. Geneviève [patron saint of Paris], for I have the impression that Paris has become receptive to her intercession; not only because of the danger that threatens, but also because the eternal problems have drawn nigh to the life of this world down here, and consequently, the saints have drawn nigh unto us.

Dear Fr. Sergius, tell me about yourself! How are you? May God keep you. I embrace you with all my affection.

Your priest Dimitri.

How would Fr. Dimitri get along with Mother Maria? Of course, that was the big question. He was much younger than she, lacking experience, as reserved as she was extroverted. But he already knew Mother Maria—they had met at the RSCM congresses and followed the same routes of exile. In a certain way, their characters were complementary and they got along right away. Comforted, Metropolitan Eulogius would later say, "The credit was all due to Fr. Dimitri, who was gifted with a rare quality—a total absence of love of self."[2]

Of course, this does not mean that Mother Maria and Fr. Dimitri always agreed on everything; there are several indications that confirm this. Sometimes, Mother Maria's outbursts would vex Fr. Dimitri. The nun loved provocation. When the prefecture officials came to Lourmel to put up posters with an appeal to go to Germany under the auspices of the Mandatory Work Service, she immediately and in plain sight tore them down, without even waiting for the officials to be gone. As for Fr. Dimitri, he preferred conspiracy. He did not seek to be a hero, but acted with discretion.

An account from this period reveals well the difference in temperament and the way in which the priest was able occasionally to put the nun in her place. One day, Mother Maria was reading in a loud voice— and with visible approval—a proclamation issued by the Resistance: the vengeance that would be taken against collaborators with the Germans was announced. Fr. Dimitri said to her softly, "Don't you think that there is already enough suffering without having to dream up yet more vengeance?" Sophie Koulomzin, who recalls the incident, affirms that Mother Maria blushed and fell silent.

Nonetheless, for the most part Fr. Dimitri worked hand in hand with Mother Maria, taking part in all her activities and in those of Orthodox Action, which envisioned itself as an organization in service of the poor. Later, when they were arrested, he energetically refused to dissociate himself from her and assumed the consequences—even to death.

2   Homily given in 1944 by Metropolitan Eulogius at a meeting dedicated to Fr. Dimitri's memory. Published in Russian in *Le Messager (Vestnik)* vol. 168 (1993), pp. 86–89, and in the book *Life and Vita of Priest Dimitri Klepinin* (YMCA Press-Russky Put', 2004 [in Russian]).

# Lourmel: Lively Disorder ❧

❧ TO WHAT COULD WE COMPARE LOURMEL? TO PROVIDE some background, I am going to have recourse above all to memories from a later period. We returned there, in fact, after the war—the building was not torn down until the 1970s. Close bonds had been formed among most of the parishioners, some of whom, such as the Babadzhan and Vnorovsky families, still lived in the house. The Vnorovskys had a daughter my age, Anna, but I was afraid to visit her because they had a pet rat! The Russian school was still in operation on Thursdays [a day off for French schools] and Anna Chumkina, a friend of my mother's whom she had met in Latvia, put on performances which we attended from time to time, in spite of the fact that Mother was reluctant to go where so many tragic events had unfolded.

Lourmel was a huge house which had certainly known a certain opulence at one time in that quarter of Grenelle. Built on two levels with a decorative façade in the style of the Second Empire, a roof over the mezzanine, it must have belonged to a wealthy merchant or to a noble family that used the courtyard for its stable and its common area. Having fallen into a state of great neglect, it had been on the market for a long time before Mother Maria came to look at it.

When she discovered it, the nun had foreseen, with her innate artistic sense, that she could use its eighteen bedrooms for her dream of a great shelter for homeless families. The best surprise was in particular the room for lectures and for dining, which she could not organize on that scale in the previous house, the Villa de Saxe, which was too cramped. She told Konstantin Mochulsky[1] enthusiastically, "At Villa de Saxe, I fed twenty-five people. At Lourmel I can maintain a hundred!"

So Mother Maria moved in there in 1934. Overflowing with energy, she had converted and transformed various parts of the house, pulled up the old linoleum that covered the floor, brought to light an old hardwood floor which she fussed over and sanded and waxed. The stalls were removed from the stable and it was turned into a chapel. Fr. Lev Gillet[2] was the first priest to celebrate there. He, too, left the Villa de Saxe and came to occupy a simple bedroom in the common area.

All sorts of people stayed at Lourmel. There were families whose father worked in a factory or as a cab driver. Alexis Babadzhan, a close friend of our family, was a lab assistant at the Pasteur Institute, where he was in charge of taking care of the mice, a detail that made a big impression on me. His wife worked for a fashion designer. Olga Tatarinova's family stayed, all three of them, in what would later be our family's room in the attic. Their mother had been a doctor in Russia, and the two sisters were learning to type while they worked here and there as maids. The painter Nadezhda Veryovkina lived briefly at Lourmel and in gratitude for Mother Maria's help, did a beautiful portrait of her, striking in its truth, portraying her as she typed.

All the people who lived at Lourmel had known better days in Russia. Most of them tried to remain dignified in spite of the shakiest financial situation. Some of them cooked in their rooms over Godin burners which were intended to heat their quarters. Since there was no running water, it had to be carried in pitchers. The dining room opened at noon. They could take some mess tins and dish out their food. On Thursdays the house was full of laughter from the children of the Russian school.

But what remains above all in the collective memory of the former residents of Lourmel is the sort of disorder that ruled there. As Fr. Lev Gillet described it, there was "a sort of pandemonium" in which "bums,

---

1   Konstantin Mochulsky (1892–1948), a literary critic, was a member of Orthodox Action.

2   Father Lev Gillet (1893–1980), who signed his works "A Monk of the Eastern Church," carried out his ministry in Paris and London. A prolific author, he is one of the major figures of contemporary Orthodox spirituality. See Elisabeth Behr-Sigel, *Un moine de l'Eglise d'Orient (A Monk of the Eastern Church)*, Paris, Editions du Cerf, 1993.

streetwalkers, and the Benedictine choir of Dom Malherbe were mixed together." One episode illustrates this impression of the court of miracles—one night the cook Mitrophan came back drunk to Lourmel and mistakenly entered the room of Fr. Lev Gillet, who woke up startled and cried out, "On guard!"

Before the war, Lourmel was a place that was known to everyone who was in difficulty—those who did not have their papers in order, who had no work permit, no place to stay, no money. Mother Maria had opened a social service center, a kitchen. The parish functioned at full speed. The Russians found consolation and support there. There were many burials, because the hearses could enter the courtyard. Mother Maria had the idea then of embroidering the names of the deceased on a huge white banner decorated with angels, which she hung above the so-called "canon's" table where the *panikhidas*[3] were celebrated.

That was when the war broke out. Foreseeing it, Mother Maria had gathered provisions, and the household did not disperse. Life at Lourmel continued in spite of the horrors of the situation and the persecutions of the Jews that began before long. The house was crammed full of people on a permanent basis.

3   Services for the dead.

# Priesthood as Self-Offering ⚭

⚭ THE PRECIOUS DATEBOOK REVEALS ANOTHER DESIRE THAT is very characteristic for a young priest—that of building. Fr. Dimitri sketched in his notebook some carpenter's tools—plane and compass saw—and noted the French words for them. At Lourmel he wanted to build a side altar to celebrate early liturgy there. In the courtyard adjoining the chapel there is a little place Mother Maria had in mind as a confessional, but Fr. Dimitri did not find it very accommodating. The idea of installing an altar there dedicated to St. Philip, Metropolitan of Moscow, preoccupied him more and more.

Why this saint in particular? Fr. Dimitri's friend and professor at St. Sergius, the historian George Fedotov, had just published a book on him, a providentially written biography in those times of rampant totalitarianism. In the sixteenth century, in fact, Ivan IV (Ivan the Terrible) sowed terror in Russia with his "black guard," which ravaged the Russian province and indulged in all sorts of exactions. One man alone resisted, the boyar Philip Kolychev, whom the tsar had brought back from the Solovki Islands where, as a young abbot, he had considerably reestablished the local monastic community and had created a flourishing economy. Promoted to metropolitan of Moscow, Philip dared to oppose the tsar, exhorting him to be more gentle. Ivan did not put up with it. He dismissed the prelate and exiled him to a monastery, but Philip continued to send the tsar appeals to be moderate and charitable. At that point Ivan signed a death warrant for Philip and had him strangled in his cell. St. Philip's approach appeared to be Fr. Dimitri's in that first year of the war[1]—to have the daring to resist a tyrant.

Fr. Dimitri committed himself fully not only to his new priestly ministry but also to Lourmel. He organized evening lectures for the elderly persons who frequented the house and training courses for readers and chanters. To what could we compare Fr. Dimitri's pastoral work? To describe it, I will employ the moving testimony of one of his parishioners, Maria Kravchenko:

> Fr. Dimitri was extraordinarily simple, with that particular sort of simplicity that is found only in wisdom. He greeted everyone as simply and easily as children do. It is not that he was unaware of evil, but he brushed it aside consciously, placing the center of gravity on what was better, what was possible, what was not yet brought to reality and yet given.
>
> On first meeting him, I encountered a man of medium height with a black beard, dressed in a cassock, who walked toward us as we came down Olivier de Serres street. When he reached us, he cast us an amused look and passed by. Who is that? The new priest? Who is he? One day, by chance, I went to him to confess and I was quickly taken by his simplicity and sweetness. At that time I was going through a particularly difficult situation and he undertook my healing. His treatment consisted in turning me away from my misfortune by pointing out someone who was even more unfortunate, and insisting that I should take active steps to help someone else. That was when I made the acquaintance of an authentic Russian [children's] nurse, a marvelous woman who had been brought to Paris by a rich merchant from Moscow. She was illiterate, and it was in serving this Russian nurse that I was employed by Fr. Dimitri, which brought us close together. He was pleased with this friendship and laughed good-heartedly at my stories about her. I remember a discussion we had about her. I was saying that the nurse had a hard time expressing herself and understanding the world around her, but he retorted that lowly people have, on the contrary, a simple manner of viewing things and that surely she felt more comfortable with the doorkeeper, the shopkeeper, or the cobbler than a Russian intellectual would with his French equivalent.

[1]  For the same reasons, Philip of Moscow was also the saint most venerated by Fr. Alexander Men. See in particular Alexander Men, *Le christianisme ne fait que commencer,* Paris et Pully, Editions du Cerf-sel de la terre, 1996, pp. 78–82.

I also remember how Fr. Dimitri helped me save an alcoholic who was tangled up in his sins and despair. He watched for him at night at the doorway of his hotel, standing at the coachman's door. He looked over this sick man carefully and sweetly, with friendship and love. He gave him holy water to drink and brought him prosphora, but he did not admit him to communion "until his passions calmed down." We celebrated some molebens for his healing, and it ended up happening. The beginning of his cure coincided with Transfiguration, a feast which Fr. Dimitri particularly loved.

Fr. Dimitri was very intelligent. It seems to me that the cast of his mind was Socratic. He responded simply to the most difficult questions, often with a question in return, and his reply stuck in the memory.

He never lectured anyone or reproached them. He seemed to make excuses for the sins of his flock and showed the same tender and constant love toward them all. Exacting toward himself, he was extraordinarily benevolent towards others. He did not place an unbearable burden on anyone, did not require the impossible, did not punish, but bore witness to mercy. In all the time I spent in his company, I never heard him condemn anyone, nor even grow irritated or show frustration toward anyone.

He made himself available to an incredible degree. At every moment, this man who was so busy would tear himself away from his many obligations and run to someone's aid. I see the two of us running together to the hospital where there lies the still-warm body of a dear friend. His death devastates me, I am overwhelmed by grief, I weep and ask Fr. Dimitri, "Where is he now?" And the father answers, "Who knows?" We leave again and still in tears, I say, "And if he isn't anywhere?" He replies calmly and distinctly, as if to a child, "He is certainly somewhere!" Suddenly I calm down and my tears are no longer so bitter. In these dark days Fr. Dimitri never leaves me. He prays, he sustains me and, with his help, death is covered with light.

I saw him again in the street, announcing to me with great joy that he has been appointed to Lourmel Street, to Mother Maria's. The prospect of creative work brought him joy. I told him, "What rich human material is going to pass through your hands! You will have to take notes." He replied that, alas, he would not have time.

Those who have rubbed shoulders with him know what a gigantic task this fragile man has accomplished. This huge and difficult parish with its physical and spiritual needs and its complex human relationships rested on his shoulders. This man, who had no rest, would accuse himself to his spiritual children of laziness, of negligence, of forgetfulness, of carelessness, when there was not a single example of someone he did not try to help, no sick person he had not visited, no parishioner whose life he did not know in detail. He insisted on the fact that it was necessary not only to help them morally, but also materially, that a hungry man has a hard time understanding abstractions. How he worried over the joyless existence of the old people who lived at the home! How he reproached himself for not being able to spend more time with them, at least to make them laugh.

During the years of war, persecutions, and trials, Fr. Dimitri was a support to many and he saved more than one. "If a man surprised by a storm takes shelter in a church, do I have the right to close the door?" he would say when someone asked him, "Are you sure these people are sincere?" Or again, "When a man who is being hounded is knocking at your door hoping to be saved, do you ask who he is?"

At the time of a meeting of the circle where he was explaining the liturgy, I remember his astonishingly clear and simple commentary on the words "an offering of peace, a sacrifice of praise"—that the best sacrifice humanity can offer God is an offering of love. Fr. Dimitri manifested this love completely. It is not by chance that he had carved on the doors of the church these words which can be considered as his motto: "Unite, Lord, all those who communicate in Your body and Your blood."[2]

Many parishioners have retold the story of Pascha night of 1942 at Lourmel. "Outside there were restrictions, anguish, war. Here in the church lit up by our candles, was our priest, all vested in white, as if borne on the wings of the winds. With his face radiant he proclaimed, 'Christ is risen!' And we responded, 'Truly, He is risen!' causing the shadows to scatter."

My last image of my father is that last Eucharist he celebrated at Lourmel in the church of the Protection of the Mother of God. After that liturgy, in my childish imagination, he set the chalice on the altar, drew the curtain, and went to be with the Father.

---

2   From the Divine Liturgy of St. Basil, immediately following the Consecration of the Gifts.

At that period, quite clearly I was unaware of that intense pastoral activity on my father's part, because I was still just a little girl, happy, and besides, I was kept carefully from the worries and horrors of the time. All the same, some memories have remained with me, which were inevitably just bits and pieces, but still infinitely precious. I would like to evoke them now.

Belgrade, New Year, 1925. Right to left: Nicolas Zernov, unknown, Tatiana Klepinin, Dmitri Klepinin, Maria Zernov, Andrey Klepinin, unknown, Igor Troianov

Paris, 1925. St. Sergius Theological Institute. First row, left to right: Fr. George Shumkin, Fr. Leon Zander, Sergei Bezobrazov, Anton Kartashev, Fr. Sergei Bulgakov, Metropolitan Evlogii, Bishop Benjamin, unknown, Vladimir Ilzhin, Peter Kovalevsky. Dmitri Klepinin is standing behind Ilzhin.

Above: Summer camp of the RSCM, around 1930. Dmitri is standing on the left, Basil Zenkovsky in the middle. Fr. Sergei Chetverikov is sitting on the right, and at his left is Sophie Shidlovksy.

Below: Dmitri and Tamara at a summer conference of RSCM, June 1937.

Fr. Dimitri, Paris, 1939.

Paris, 1937–38. First parish at the headquarters of the RSCM. The rector, Fr. Sergei Chetverikov, is in the middle, Fr. Dimitri at his left. Standing: Fr. George Serikov.

Rue de Lourmel, October 1939. Left to right: Sophie Pilenko, Yuri Skobtsov, Alexis Babadzhan, Mother Maria, George Fedotov, Fr. Dimitri, Konstantin Mochulsky.

EGLISE ORTHODOXE

de l'Intercession de la Sainte-Vierge

77, Rue de Lourmel, Paris-15ᵉ

Extrait du registre des baptêmes

en l'année 1940

| Date | | Prénom du baptisé | Nom et prénom des parents | Nom et prénom des parrains | Qui a célébré le baptême |
|---|---|---|---|---|---|
| de naissance | de baptême | | | | |
| | | Natalie | Cyrille Roujine de religion orthodoxe et sa femme Mathéa née Cusnir | Vladimir Sipourjinsky Vera Timofeeff. | Prêtre Dimitri Klépinine |

Cet extrait a été délivré par le recteur de l'Eglise de l'Intercession de la Sainte Vierge 77 rue de Lourmel Paris XV le 16 DEC 1942 à Paris

Prêtre Dimitri Klépinine

1942. Certificate of baptism for N. Ruzhina.

Fr. Dimitri, his wife, and daughter Helen, 1940.

Above: Paul and Helen Klepinin, 1943.
Photo sent to Fr. Dimitri in prison.

Right: Tamara Klepinin and her children
in Chaville, 1943.

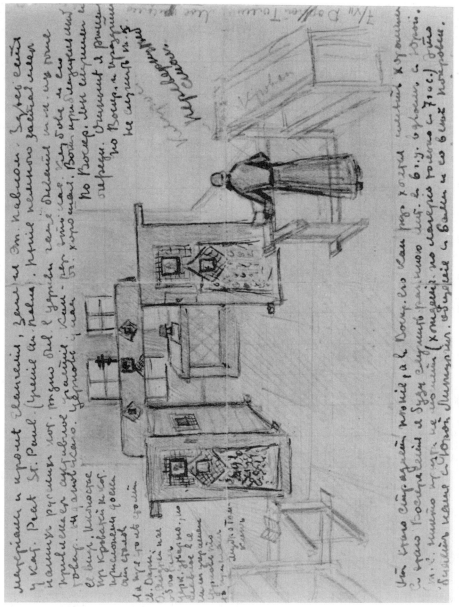

1943. Letter from Fr. Dimitri while imprisoned at Compiègne, with drawing of chapel there.

# תעודה
# ATTESTATION

## Père Dimitri Klépinine

שם  נפשו  בכפו  להצלת יהודים בתקופת השואה.

**AU PERIL DE SA VIE à SAUVE DES JUIFS PENDANT L'HOLOCAUSTE**

נטע  עץ  בשדרת חסידי אומות העולם

**à PLANTE UN ARBRE DANS L'ALLEE DES JUSTES**

LE 14 Août 1987     ביום יט אב תשמ״ז

בשם רשות הזיכרון יד־ושם     בשם הוועדה לציון חסידי אומות העולם

Pour l'Institut du Souvenir Yad Vashem     Pour la Commission des Justes

ונתתי להם בביתי ובחומותי יד ושם... אשר לא יכרת. ישעיהו נ״ו...

...JE LEUR DONNERAI UNE PLACE ET UN NOM...QUI NE PERIRA PAS... ESAIE, 56

Fr. Dimitri is honored with the title of Righteous among the Nations by the Institute Yad Vashem in Israel.

Icon of St. Dimitri.

# *Birds in Cassocks* ☙

☙ IN MY MIND LOURMEL IS ALWAYS ASSOCIATED WITH SOMEthing wintery and gray. The three of us lived in an attic room in Mother Maria's house. Naturally my papa was a priest, obviously, like all the papas in the world, even the papas among the animals. That's how I saw things at the age I began to express myself. I told little stories in Russian about a family of birds. When the table is set, baby bird flies to papa bird and tugs on his cassock: "Come and bless the meal!"

The first time I realized my mistake, we were walking down the street and met my girlfriend Nina Lavrukhina, along with her father, who was strangely enough dressed in civilian clothes. "Say hello to Nina's father, Ladushka!" The world grew larger—there were papas without cassocks.

This nickname Ladushka—was it my papa who gave it to me? Did it come to him from that tradition the Klepinins had of giving their children nicknames? This time, after all, he did not pull it out of a bestiary, but from a gesture of clapping that I was happily making with my hands. There is in fact a story that evokes that gesture—*"Ladushki, ladushki,"*—which Russian mothers chant. Then all the parishioners started calling me Ladushka, but as for Papa, he called me Ladkin or Ladik, which is masculine in Russian.

Obviously it didn't bother him. As an expression of intimacy he called his wife Tamara by the name Tomik and spoke of her in the third person and in the masculine gender. That was his way of being tender. Later in his letters from Compiègne, he used formulas such as,

"I hope my Tomkin is in bed and sleeping peacefully," or again, "You made me happy in describing Ladkin's life and how he is taking care of Pavkin." He signed his letters Sobaka and spoke of himself in the feminine! In this way he created an intimate grammar which is affectionate and amusing. If I speak of it, it is because it really is a well-founded habit among the Klepinins—my aunt did the same with her son, duly baptized Andrey, but never designated in any other way than as Kot or Masik.

How interesting a childhood memory is—in the middle of a long black patch of forgetfulness, there are such astonishingly precise areas! I see my papa again in his cassock, standing on a stool. He is holding a huge paper airplane. I hold my breath, because he is about to let it go—the white triangle twirls through the room and lands on the floor at my feet. An explosion of joy! Or again, some priest friends came up to see us. I climbed up onto my papa's knees and twisted his beard. As if I wanted to show my circle of companions how proud I was and how I had the right to be so familiar.

But I, too, have my times of pouting. The courtyard at Lourmel is full of children from the Thursday school. They come there for their catechism lesson. It's playtime and Fr. Dimitri, with his cassock unfurled, plays at being a hawk with them. But as for me, too small to join their struggles, I am told to stay on the steps across from the chapel. I am burning with jealousy, especially when the big black hawk catches one of the children and both of them laugh, carefree and happy, insensitive to my state of mind.

And then let's not forget the war with its privations, its rationing cards, its lines at the stores. My family stayed in Paris like most Russians. Where would they have gone? We had no cousins in Brittany and no villas on the coast! In case of emergency, some people took their bicycles and left on the roads to exchange their clothes for butter. My parents were assisted by the parish community and the organization in which they participated alongside Mother Maria. Orthodox Action had a kitchen and benefited from some grants from the municipality of the Fifteenth Arrondissement.

But above all there were bombing raids and sirens. When they started to howl, people threw themselves into their cellars. That was when my father invented a game that was intended to reassure me, which not only created a secret agreement between us, but it also made those sirens miraculously attractive. This begins like all tales: "Once upon a time there was a huge cat and this cat had a lo-o-o-o-o-ng tail like this," and my papa's voice would swell to the rhythm of the siren that bellowed above the dormer windows. Then one day this cat grabs a little mouse (that's me, smiling with contentment) and says, "A-a-a-ah! A mouse! I'm going to eat you!" I shuddered, but I knew that the joke was almost over. And then, it was my turn to reply, "No, big pussy-cat, don't eat me, please, I have a daddy and a mommy!" And the big cat responded, "A-a-a-ah! Is it like tha-a-a-at? Then save yourself!" Meanwhile either the siren had stopped or else the story began again. Children are so insatiable! This is why I have no bad memories of sirens.

Another reminiscence—here I am in church, which is full of my friends. All the parishioners were smiling at their priest's daughter and I felt very full of myself. Carried by my mother, who was bringing me to receive communion, I reached the level of the choir, where I had even more friends. I squirmed and tried to draw the attention of the choir members. But suddenly my papa became very serious and cast a reproving glance at me. He was holding the chalice, but stupid me, I was creating an uproar and destroying the harmony. That instant before the royal doors, that moment when I was taking communion from his hand, has remained focused and engraved in my memory as a four-year-old child.

These are pretty much all the memories I have retained of my priest-father. Mother, who tried to raise us in his memory, told me many other episodes later. She told me, for example, that he was terribly worried about the harm that could happen to us. And so one day when I banged myself on the table, he took a saw, and if Mother had not intervened, he would certainly have cut off the four corners. I no longer remember the fear I caused him by running across the street, or the spanking—the one and only one—that he gave me on that occasion.

# *Little Paul* ⌀⌀

⌀⌀ MOTHER HAS OFTEN REMINDED US THAT FR. DIMITRI WAS mad with joy to be not only a priest but also the father of a family. He was the papa of a little Helen, me, and a little Paul, who was born in 1942. That year I spent the month of August in Moisenay, in the Ile-de-France region in Mother Theodosia's convent.[1] I was four years old, and they had left me in the care of the good sisters while my mother was in Paris. In my memory there is one astonishingly precise recollection in that forgotten summer—a big fly was banging and buzzing against the window panes while tiny specks of dust danced in a sunbeam. It was summer and I daydreamed, blessed and happy. From that time on, all through my life, for me to really feel that it is summer there has to be that impalpable buzzing and whirling. I slept in a hayloft at the top of a barn. My straw mattress rustled and some wisps pricked my back, but they did nothing to interfere with my sense of peace.

And there was Mother Theodosia's blotchy face as she bent over me. "You've got a little brother, Ladushka! What a joy! A little Paul!" I knit my brows. "And Mother? what did Mother get?" The nun burst out laughing. She would repeat that reply back to me for years, even when she became abbess of the Monastery of the Protection of the Mother of God at Bussy-en-Othe in the Yonne region of Burgundy. "What did Mother get, you replied," and her beautiful face with her red cheeks would light up.

---

1   Mother Theodosia Solomiantz (1903–1998) became a nun in 1933, first in a little
    convent at Moisenay-en-Brie, then at the monastery founded by Mother Eudoxia
    at Bussy-en-Othe, where she became abbess in 1991.

They brought me to view my little brother at the clinic, but I had eyes only for Mother. She was stretched out on a bed that was so tall I could barely see her. Papa hoisted me to her side, and I stayed there snuggled against her. I put up quite a fuss when they pulled me away.

Mother used to say how proud Papa was to have a son. It was the same thing with my grandfather. He had written from Belgrade that Paul was the one who would carry on the family line, would carry on the name, since his oldest son Nikolai did not have a son. As for me, I began to include that little brother in my universe only during the year 1943 when we were living at Chaville and our father was in captivity. Paul was then beginning to babble. We had a room decorated with a frieze that ran around the ceiling and told the story of the Russian peasant uprooting an enormous turnip with the help of his wife, his daughter, his dog, his cat, and a little mouse. We knew that story by heart, and I amused myself by repeating the refrain to Pavlik, "They pulled, they pulled, but they couldn't pull it out."

I remember the anguish that would come over me when Mother would leave us by ourselves. The house was full of disturbing noises, and I had the impression that someone was coming up the stairs. In the letters Mother sent to Compiègne, she said that I was taking my role as older sister very seriously. When Paul began to walk, the privations of the war caused his legs to be crooked. We had to find him an emergency supply of vitamins. But he was a joyful and independent little boy. One day when the metal gate was left open, he went out in the street and took off on an adventure. We didn't find him again until evening. I can just imagine how worried Mother was!

Paul spoke French almost as quickly as he spoke Russian because we had Madame Aimée. What memories are connected with that woman, so devoted and so loving! She was very attached to my brother, and would call him "my little Paul." She sang songs to us and took us out to gather cherries in her garden at Chaville. She formed the bridge between our little Russian world and France. She provided an incalculable support to Mother, who was grappling with her solitude as the wife of a prisoner. When the terrible news came that Papa had died, Madame Aimée was able to find, in her fervent Protestant practice, the words to calm Mother and console her. Her husband, René Leprêtre, who also tried to console Mother, told her, "Don't worry, Madame Klepinin, you're going to be able to get a pension now as a war widow!"

# ✪ VI ✪

# *Persecution & Martyrdom*

# The Jews ❧

❧ WHAT IS HEROISM? WE OFTEN MISUNDERSTAND THIS NO-
tion, which we associate with striking brilliant action and great war-
like deeds. But there is another sort of heroism that is carried out in
the shadows and discreetly. The assistance the group at Lourmel was
about to give to the Jews was of this type. A significant detail is that it
was not until the dossier on Fr. Dimitri was turned over to the Israeli
committee of Yad Vashem towards 1984 that I learned—through the
testimony of Jews who had been saved by my father—that during the
week my mother spent in the maternity hospital, a Jewish family had
been accommodated in our room. I well remember the hidden staircase they used the day of a raid.

The pursuit of the Jews began soon after the armistice of June 1940.
On September 27, the occupation authorities published a series of de-
crees intended to register the Jewish population of France. One highly
symbolic moment was the famous raid on Vel'd'hiv, which is near the
rue de Lourmel. At the end of the war there was a count: 75,721 Jews
were deported and only 2,560 escaped. The Jews were seen by the Nazis
as a religious rather than an ethnic group. They considered someone
a Jew who either confessed or had confessed the Jewish religion or
counted at least two Jews among his grandparents. On October 3, 1940,
the Vichy government introduced the notion of the Jewish couple.

Parishioners who found themselves in danger because they were
born Jews made entreaties to the French clergy. Vichy, in fact, took no
account of their conversion to Christianity. There were some faithful

of Jewish origin among the circle of Lourmel. In the first period, Fr. Dimitri was led to provide baptismal certificates to Russians who had the misfortune of having the first name Jacob or Simon. Then he provided certificates to those who, although they were of Jewish origin, had converted, for example upon marriage with an "Aryan." This first "transgression" of my father's was soon followed by other liberties to save non-baptized Jews as well.

Our family archives include three documents of particular interest which illustrate very well the steps a Jew had to take to avoid any mention of his being Jewish on his passport. They concern the wife of the man who became the historian of the concentration camps, George Wellers. He came to Lourmel in March 1942 to ask for a baptismal certificate for his wife. Fr. Dimitri testified that Anna Wellers was a parishioner of his church. The certificate was stamped by the police commissioner of the Javel quarter. But that was not enough. It also needed the testimony of the diocese administration on rue Daru. This document is much more complete, because it mentions Anna Wellers' parents and grandparents and certifies under oath (because there were no witnesses) that all six were Orthodox Christians. This new certificate was stamped by the president of the diocesan council and the general secretary.

Armed with these two papers, Wellers went to the fearsome General Commissariat for Jewish Questions. The French functionary's reply is a model of ambiguity: "I cannot deliver you a certificate of non-appurtenance to the Jewish race, although I have determined to consider you a non-Jew." This courageous decision was sufficient to save the life of Anna Wellers and for a long time preserved her husband, "spouse of an Aryan," from deportation. He would end up being sent to Buchenwald, but returned alive.

It was George Wellers who, in gratitude, would turn over Fr. Dimitri's dossier, which would be granted the title "Righteous among the Nations" by the Israeli committee of Yad Vashem. I had the opportunity to meet George in 1985. Born in St. Petersburg in 1905, he had kept unchanged in his immense memory the remembrance of his companions who had disappeared in the extermination camps, and after his liberation he decided to dedicate all his free time to them. In 1981 he published the first work that documented the "final solution."[1] He showed

---

1  George Wellers, *Les chambres a gaz ont existé. Des documents, des temoignages, des chiffres*. Gallimard, 1981.

me a document that moved me—on the evening of their departure for Germany, some Jews detained at Drancy signed a collective letter thanking the Christians of Lourmel who sent them packages. George Wellers died in 1991.

One detail struck me in the certificate given out by the diocese—the deposition of witness statements under oath. It referred me back to the testimony of T. Imbert, who had accompanied a Jewish woman friend to see Fr. Dimitri. She was so impressed by the formula of the oath, which invoked the flames of hell on anyone who committed perjury, that she insisted on being baptized rather than asking anyone to testify falsely.

Fr. Dimitri took great risks to establish these famous certificates. To be sure that he would recognize his new flock in case he encountered them, he glued each of their photographs on a card and learned his card file by heart. It occurred to him to create biographies. When it was a matter of women married to Jewish men, he arranged to find them good Russian girls' names such as Glebova or Ivanova. One day he was threatened from an unsuspected direction—that of his own ecclesiastical authorities. Undoubtedly frightened by the number of certificates he had to deliver, a diocesan functionary demanded that the priest produce his parish registers. Fr. Dimitri simply refused. "Those who are baptized are my spiritual children, and your conduct is not inspired by spiritual considerations, but to indulge the occupation authorities. The Church has always been a place of sanctuary for victims of barbarism. No, I will not let you see my parish registers."

Mother certainly participated in this scheme of baptismal certificates delivered to true and false Christians whose only wrong was to be called Silberstein or Lourie. Not only was she perfectly in the know, but she served as their godmother if things came to that point. One day when she saw that some of the baptismal certificates were marked in pencil with the letter "t," at first she thought it had to do with her own goddaughters or those of her sister-in-law Tatiana. But Fr. Dimitri, adopting an attitude which was at once mysterious and amused, replied to her that the letter "t" designated for him alone the false baptismal certificates. It referred to the French word *tilleul* (lime tree), which was translated in Russian by *lipa*, which, in a figurative sense, meant "substitute" or "ersatz." It was his humorous way of engaging in conspiracy.

"No, I am not a heroine," Mother told me later. "The only thing I can be proud of is that I never tried to turn your father aside from his dangerous activity. I never told him not to put our family in danger, contrary to what the Soviet novelist Elena Mikulina claims in her book *Mother Maria.*"

One day Fr. Dimitri admitted to his friends that he was afraid. How many certificates had he drawn up saying that people belonged to his parish, and how many Jews had he baptized? Today no one can say. In an interview with a Jewish journalist, Lydia Blicher, Mother spoke about a hundred or so cards. What was admirable was that Fr. Dimitri was not content to help the people who presented themselves to him, but he himself went to people's houses when he knew they were in danger. This was the case of the very young Natasha Ruzhina. He was the one who went to find her and who brought her in her crib all the way across Paris to hide her at Lourmel. She told the story in a newspaper in Moldova, where she lived. Her family saved as a precious relic the Gospel book the priest gave her, in which he had written on the flyleaf, "Come to Me, all you who labor, and I will give you rest."

# The Raid in February  &ෝ

&ෝ *D*ARK HOURS CAME THEN TO LOURMEL. BETWEEN THE eighth and the twelfth of February, 1943, the Gestapo showed up and arrested the whole group—Mother Maria, her son Yuri, Fr. Dimitri, Theodore Pianov, George Kazachkin, and even poor Anatoly, a mentally ill man who helped Mother Maria in the kitchen. I can see myself on the day of the first raid sitting on my bed next to the door. Mother was bent over the Godin stove, stirring it and feverishly burning some heaps of paper. We heard sounds of boots on the stairs and suddenly she closed the stove. A German officer came in. He had a stare like blue steel and spoke German with Mother. I could feel my anguish grow in me, and I saw nothing but that hostile military man. Later I learned that his name was Hoffman and that he had come to arrest my papa, whom I would never see again. Mother told me that my brother's diapers were full of banknotes intended for Jewish families that the Lourmel group was helping.

The hours grew even darker. I was separated from Mother, who had to leave Lourmel suddenly and take refuge with friends she could trust. In fact the Nazis continued their forays at the house, and Hoffman told her that he was coming back to pay special attention to her. Alas!—her emotions had shaken her. She had jaundice, and they put me in a boarding school at La Ferté-Allais. I have retained even more memories of that sad page of my life, when I was as unhappy as could be—the trial must have made me grow up. In particular, I see myself lying down in the bathtub pressing the sponge Mother had given me against my nose. It still smelled like the house, and I cherished it as my only ally. The kitchen of the boarding house, on the other hand, was dominated by the odor of war rations—rutabagas, which I detest, and sticky cold noodles.

But what comes back to me above all is the feeling of a great solitude. I didn't know French, and the other children struck me as hostile, like the world outside. Something broke inside me—I was walking through a meadow full of daffodils, and suddenly I fell and forgot everything. Undoubtedly I had fallen ill and they had to take care of me . . . The only thing I remember is that cold sunny morning when Mother came to pick me up again. I was outside, I had my rabbit-skin slippers on my feet, all soaked from the rain; Mother stretched out her arms to me and I rushed toward her with happiness and desolation.

La Ferté-Allais is also linked with the memory of my pretty Aunt Tanya. She, like her brother Fr. Dimitri, was involved in the Resistance. When she was hunted by the Gestapo, she put my cousin Andrey, four years old, in the same boarding house with me. So then I had an ally in the place, except that he seemed to be very much at home there. Of course!—he had a Russian friend nicknamed Fiou, and above all his mother was nearby. She was staying in the inn of the village, where she took shelter when the threat of arrest became apparent. On Sundays during that period of time I would go to meet her in that little house, where I certainly must have spent the night from time to time, because I saw my aunt undress and brush her long hair, which fell over her nightgown. These were moments of happiness like those captured in those rare photos I have at hand. I was all smiles in the light of spring in 1943, in Tanya's arms alongside Andrey. All that—thoughtless childhood!—right when Papa was confined in the camp at Compiègne and saw them leave, one after the other, his companions who were deported for the German work camps or extermination camps.

Later on, Judith Kazachkina—whom we call "Iudinka" and whose husband shared Papa's fate—told me of an episode that is linked to La Ferté-Allais. She, a Jewish woman, forced to wear the yellow star, had a chance to slip through the net. First she hid at Lyons, then in the region of Paris where the Klepinins—Tanya as well as Mother—offered her hospitality. Our two families have, in fact, closer ties than those of blood in the banal sense. We will be tied together forever by that shared blood of martyrdom. Although he was "Aryan," George Kazachkin was arrested because he ran to Lourmel the day he learned about the arrest of his friend Fr. Dimitri, to help his godson Paul, my little brother. George was being held at Compiègne, then, for the crime of compassion, and Judith went into hiding.

She came to Ferté to spend a few days with Tanya. Suddenly the innkeeper burst into the room and warned the two women, "The Krauts are here!" Tanya quickly proposed a daring plan—as quietly as possible, Judith would take little Andrey by the hand and cross the courtyard toward the toilets. What could be more natural? Beyond the recess, there was a vegetable garden which opened out onto a path through the forest. They could stay there until the "Krauts" had gone. Tanya reassured Judith. Her false papers were very convincing, and the innkeeper would not inform on her—he liked her and hated the Krauts.

The plan was a success. After spending several hours in the forest, Judith made it back to the inn. My cousin must have felt the danger they were running, because before pushing open the gate, Judith hesitated, and Andrey started trembling. "I'm afraid, Iudinka, I'm afraid, you know?" Poor Judith was in a tight corner, too, but good fortune was on her side. In this way, she was able once again to escape the raid.

# The Camp at Compiègne-Royallieu ᴏ҉

ᴏ҉ WE WERE AT LA FERTÉ-ALLAIS, THEN, WHILE FR. DIMITRI and his companions were confined. "I helped as well as I could . . ." Mother would say later, more than modest. During her husband's captivity, in fact, she conducted herself like a true heroine. "When your father was arrested, I moved heaven and earth to tear him out of the claws of the Gestapo," she recounted. With friends who remained in Paris, she got the help of a certain Rev. Peters, a German who was interested in Orthodoxy. In fact he did intervene. They asked Fr. Dimitri to sign a declaration in exchange for his liberation, by which he would dissociate himself from the work of Mother Maria. Fr. Dimitri simply refused. The interview with the police turned sour.

"You're helping the Yids!" SS Hoffman shouted at him.

Fr. Dimitri corrected him, "No, I am helping Jews." Then showing him his pectoral cross, he added, "And this Jew here, do you know Him?"

A slap knocked him to the ground. With his cassock covered with stains, his hair completely awry, he had to pass before a group of Nazi secretaries who mocked him. Yuri, a witness of the scene, began crying. "Don't cry. Think about what Jesus suffered during His Passion," Fr. Dimitri told him.

While she had placed Paul and me in a safe place at La Ferté-Allais, Mother could not leave Paris because Fr. Dimitri was confined at

Romainville near the Porte des Lilas quarter of Paris. She went there regularly to leave packages of food and clothing. In that place of detention, the prisoners felt that they were still close to their families. From time to time they were summoned for interrogation at the Parisian Gestapo headquarters. The regime seemed endurable. They had permission to get together and to circulate between the men's sector and the women's. In this way, Mother Maria could see her son and attend the services celebrated by Fr. Mikhail Belsky.[1]

Those who were detained, however, were very poorly nourished, and hunger quickly made itself felt. They searched through the rubbish for edible peelings. One day, as Theodore Pianov tells the story, Fr. Dimitri found an onion. Happy as could be, he got ready to use it in his evening soup, but he ran into a Serb who was dying of hunger and gave it to him. As soon as the first packages arrived, he shared them with those who had not received anything.

One very cold day, my mother Tamara had the idea of bringing him a thermos with hot coffee. By chance the package was given to the prisoner the same day. Fr. Dimitri was moved to tears. More than the coffee itself—as he wrote in a letter—what touched him was that his wife had been so close to him and that the thermos had kept "the warmth of the house."

For five weeks, Tamara remained without any news of the prisoner. On February 27, 1943, Fr. Dimitri was transferred along with his companions from the fort of Romainville to Camp Royallieu, at Compiègne in the Oise region of France. Their detention there would last about eight months. Thanks to this displacement, the detained could measure the extent of the arrests during that winter of 1942 to 1943. In fact the camp was immense. The huge barracks in parallel rows covered a vast perimeter on the outskirts of the city of Compiègne, whose first buildings they could see beyond Sector C. From June 1941 to August 1944, 63,000 men, women, and children were confined, deported, and even shot at Compiègne.

The little Lourmel group found itself in rooms with fifty bunk beds each on two or three levels. The day began with roll call. The prisoners of each barrack had to line up before the German officer, who counted them. Compiègne was a transit camp, and the prisoners were not required to do any work. Time dragged out there endlessly while

1   Orthodox priest who died in 1964 and who also took part in saving Jews.

they waited for food to be distributed at noon and in the evening. Idleness, lack of privacy, and permanent hubbub generated disputes and conflicts.

Fr. Dimitri saw the advantage he could draw from that forced inactivity among his companions in misfortune. There were fifteen Russians, some Serbs, some Georgians, and some Greeks, just so many Orthodox for whom he felt responsible. Out of a concern that they eat their meals in an atmosphere of peace, he insisted that they begin and end with a prayer. He organized courses in religious instruction. For that purpose he made use of some precious books—the two volumes of Prat[2]—a commentary on the Gospels in the best tradition of Catholic biblical exegesis, written by a Jesuit father, Ferdinand Prat, and the Bible with the commentary of Louis-Claude Fillion. Fr. Dimitri also got to know his Catholic colleagues, with whom he would share their books and their skills.

Prayer meetings in French were organized as well as a liturgy in Greek. A little Orthodox choir was formed, which gave a concert of religious music. The priest obtained permission to use the Catholic facilities to celebrate liturgy. But what would he have to do to have sent to him the liturgical items and the antimension,[3] which were necessary for the celebration? It was absolutely necessary to establish a relationship by correspondence with his wife. For the moment, those who were detained had the right only to one short letter a month, which had to pass through the censors.

Fortunately, Fr. Dimitri discovered the existence of the American sector. From the beginning of the Occupation, Compiègne had received some Anglo-American detainees. They enjoyed a freer regime, and secret contacts were established between the sectors. It was a breath of fresh air for the group of Russians. Around a month after they arrived, they were able to transmit clandestine notes to their families through the American sector[4] of the camp, thanks to the intervention of Andrey Morozov, who was an engineer at a firm in Compiègne. Written either

2  Ferdinand Prat, *Jesus Christ: His Life, His Teaching and His Work,* Milwaukee, 1950.
3  Linen cloth containing relics and adorned with a representation of the placing of the Savior in the tomb, which is unfolded during the eucharistic celebration and on which the holy gifts are placed.
4  There were Anglo-Americans detained in the camp from the beginning of the Occupation. They enjoyed better conditions of detention and agreed to transmit messages that came from the French sector of the immense barracks.

in ink or in pencil on silk paper, these missives were sent to Paris. This was how my mother received around twenty letters, which constitute the *de facto* chronicle of Compiègne.[5] She did not destroy them as her husband advised her to do, but kept them as something precious. She even authorized the publication of several extracts.[6]

An overwhelming hymn to love and hope, these letters are an inestimable testimony about that period of captivity. Not only do they reflect the preoccupations of the little group of Russian prisoners that surrounded Fr. Dimitri, but they are also a gripping clarification of his personality and his pastoral activity, the mirror of his soul and his heart, which bled day and night for his family, who were given over to the thousand dangers of war.

In the course of his eight months at Compiègne, the daily liturgy was at the center of Fr. Dimitri's life. There was not a single letter that did not mention it. "Consider our separation as my being sent on a mission," he wrote. "I celebrate liturgy, I preach, I hear confessions"—he even celebrated a baptism. When he was transferred to another barrack, he set up a makeshift chapel with beds turned on end. "We feel like we are in a monastery." Metropolitan Eulogius sent an antimension, and my mother arranged to send a chalice and a paten, prosphora, and candles. This daily morning liturgy was a true comfort and a mystical link with his parishioners who remained in Paris, whose names he mentioned during the preparation of the holy gifts. The circle that studied the Gospel allowed him to strengthen the bonds between his companions. Several Soviet detainees observed these prayers and meetings from up close. After a few weeks, Fr. Dimitri succeeded in establishing contact with them.

His main concern was to reassure and console his wife. He did so with all his tenderness, all his humor, and all the love that filled him. At the same time, though, he was prepared for the inescapable. He insisted on it loudly and clearly—whatever steps she undertook with the authorities to gain his freedom, his wife must not "dissociate him from Mother Maria and Orthodox Action, because that would prejudice all our work and justify the accusations." He insisted on assuming all the responsibility for it. This was quite heroic, because he knew that

5   These letters are reproduced in the final section of this work.
6   *Vestnik*, No. 168, Paris, 1993. No. VIII of the review *Hristianos* in Riga published large extracts in Russian in 1999.

Mother Maria had been deported to Ravensbrück in April 1943. He suspected that her fate had been sealed. He turned himself over entirely to the will of God and urged his wife Tamara to adopt the same attitude. "Make the morose thoughts go away with the Jesus prayer, take communion as often as possible." In December, when he learned that he was going to be deported to Germany, he wrote, "I fully aware that the will of God is being carried out and that a new obedience in the Church is beginning for me."

These letters also testify to his constant preoccupation with ensuring a minimum material basis for his life and that of his companions in misfortune. The list of products to send is eloquent—vegetables, butter, dry biscuits, canned meat, fur-lined gloves, woolen underwear, long stockings, sandals, insoles, flints, tobacco, ink, good-quality paper, and also money. Not to forget what he needs as a priest—incense, candles, wine, oil, necessary utensils to prepare the holy gifts, icons, books to use for prayers, works to distribute, a tuning fork, and an altar cross.

Tamara did not manage to obtain all these necessary objects and foodstuffs by her own efforts. In those times of restrictions, she had to move heaven and earth and display all her ingenuity. She encouraged her husband, sent him photos of the children, tirelessly put together packages, without which the prisoners would be condemned to die of hunger. More admirable still, she served as an agent to transmit money for other prisoners, playing her role as matushka out to the end. Fr. Dimitri, in fact, multiplied his demands for help for his companions who had no family, and cited the names and prisoner numbers of those who had not received packages, so that the Lourmel committee would take charge of them. "Try to arrange so that the prisoners in the following list receive some additional food." Or again, "Such and such is literally dying of hunger, he cannot swallow anything but milk. Ask the committee to send him some powdered or concentrated milk." "Such and such was sent to Germany. Let his wife know."

Fortunately Fr. Dimitri was not alone in fighting against adversity. He was sustained by his close friends, Theodore Pianov, whom he asked to speak to him about the Russian people whom he admitted he knew poorly; and George Kazachkin, whom he affectionately called Keifer and whose cheerful character he admired as well as his qualities as an organizer, who had been worthy of being designated head man of the barracks. Above all, there was young Yuri Skobtsov, Mother Maria's son, for whom Fr. Dimitri felt a completely paternal affection and whom he was preparing for the priesthood.

Unfortunately there was also a person at Compiègne who constituted a real trial for that little group of friends—a priest who was also named Dimitri, Fr. Sobolev. He was a controversial personality. "The presence of Fr. Dimitri is a trial that was possibly sent us on purpose so that we would learn that we should always find a spiritual solution to our difficulties," he wrote. With barely concealed terms he evokes the suffering that difficult relationship provoked in him: "I pray the Lord to help us find the right approach to take with Fr. Dimitri."

Over the course of the summer, another priest came and joined them, Fr. Andrey Galkin-Vrassky. This former engineer, who came into the Resistance through the Alliance Reseau network, was ordained priest in the jurisdiction of the Russian Church Outside Russia[7] and then passed into the Moscow Patriarchate. There was a rumor circulating about him, however, that he was an agent of the British secret service. He said that he had taken a trip to the USSR, where he said he had a lot of friends.

Fr. Sobolev welcomed Fr. Vrassky as a colleague belonging to the same jurisdiction as himself, and they ousted my father from the altar, arguing that he was not from the same "shop" as they. Pianov remarked that during liturgies his friend was content to sing in the choir, and he grew worried—he, too, belonged to the so-called Moscow church, but he was outraged by the attitude of the two priests. He explained himself vigorously with them, and this had the effect of reestablishing a peace accord. Fr. Dimitri could celebrate once again. He was all the happier in that he appreciated Fr. Andrey for his dynamism. They agreed to divide the work of catechesis. Little by little Fr. Andrey, who had a lot of "people skills," became the mouthpiece for the Russian group in contact with the camp authorities. Meanwhile the

---

7   The Church known as the Russian Orthodox Church Outside Russia or the Karlovtsian Church is part of the Orthodox Church of the emigration, which, for political reasons, broke its ties with the Moscow Patriarchate and then later, with another jurisdiction—directed by Metropolitan Eulogius—which had placed itself under the jurisdiction of the Ecumenical Patriarch of Constantinople. The Church Outside Russia has tended to display very conservative, nationalist, and anti-ecumenical positions. In 2007 it reestablished eucharistic unity with the Moscow Patriarchate.

rumors about Fr. Andrey reached Metropolitan Eulogius, who decided to forbid Fr. Dimitri Klepinin to concelebrate with him.

Fr. Dimitri was appalled at the decision. How could he accept seeing a punishment fall on a man in prison who had been given no opportunity to defend himself? He wrote to Tamara, "Explain to the Metropolitan that in the conditions of our life, the most important moment is our liturgical communion and that it is a grave thing to destroy this union." It was even the more sad for him, given that he was beyond all jurisdictional divisions and he accepted all Orthodox at the eucharistic table, wherever they came from. He understood that the metropolitan was influenced by his entourage, and he denounced that "band of cowardly toadies." In a letter to his metropolitan, he defended his companion in misfortune. We can suppose that the three priests disregarded the prohibition and continued to celebrate together. Fr. Andrey suffered the same fate as his companion—he was deported to Buchenwald and died in February 1944.

The diocesan situation bothered the prisoners a great deal, because an important piece of news had just reached them. In the midst of the war, on September 8, 1943, Stalin authorized a meeting of a council of Russian bishops in Moscow. They elected Metropolitan Sergius (Starogorodsky) as Patriarch of Moscow and All Russia, with one stroke reestablishing the patriarchate. This council distributed a pastoral letter "to the Christians of the whole world" calling them to join forces to defeat Hitlerism. Informed of this new fact, the prisoners of Compiègne hoped that their metropolitan, Metropolitan Eulogius, would reunite with Moscow.

This hope was all the easier to understand given that the right-wing émigrés did not hide their sympathy for the Germans, in whom they saw providential liberators who would clear out from Russia "the atheistic Communist hydra." This, in particular, was the position of Metropolitan Anthony Khrapovitsky, the founder of the Russian Orthodox Church Outside Russia, and Archbishop Anastasius Gribanovsky, of the same jurisdiction. In 1938, the latter had sent Hitler a telegram to thank him for the help he had given to the Orthodox parishes of Germany and to assure him of his constant prayers. Metropolitan Seraphim Lukianov, who also belonged to the Church Outside Russia and whose pro-Nazi sympathies were well known, tried in 1943 to reconcile with Metropolitan Eulogius. These pieces of news disturbed the prisoners all the more because they arrived in unequivocal fashion via the only magazine authorized by the censors, *Parizhsky Vestnik (The Parisian Messenger)*, published by the pro-Nazi Yuri Zherebkov.[8] Fr. Dimitri was very worried. He hoped that his beloved metropolitan would be able to keep his independence in relation to the conservative collaborationists and that he would seize the opportunity to regain the bosom of the Moscow mother Church.

Today we know how this story turned out. In 1945, in the euphoria of victory, Metropolitan Eulogius did in fact request to be reattached to Moscow. He died in 1946. In the meantime, Patriarch Sergius had died eight months previously, just after his election, and his successor Alexis I committed the error of naming—as successor to Metropolitan Eulogius—Metropolitan Seraphim Lukianov, who, after the liberation, concerned to receive pardon for his numerous compromises with the Nazis, pledged allegiance to the Moscow Patriarchate. This nomination antagonized the majority of his Parisian diocese against Moscow and, led by Metropolitan Vladimir (Tikhonitsky), they went back under the shepherd's staff of the patriarch of Constantinople.

8  Yuri Zherebkov, nicknamed "the Russian Führer," exercised his talents at social dancing in Germany. Having joined the Nazi Party, he saw himself nominated in 1940 to the position of Gauleiter (responsible) for the Russian émigrés in France. From that point on, all the Russians were summoned to register at his office. In this way he instigated the arrest of many persons who were active in the emigration. When, at the end of 1944, the Germans authorized the foundation of the Russian Committee of Liberation presided over by General Vlassov, Zherebkov became its delegate to the German Minister of Foreign Affairs. After the defeat of Germany, Zherebkov hid in Spain, then in South America, where all trace of him was lost.

# *The Refuge of Chaville* ৩৩

৩৩ MOTHER FINALLY RECOVERED FROM HER HEPATITIS, BUT she didn't know where she wanted to live. That was when Sophie Koulomzin, whose husband Nikita had gotten a job in the country, offered her house at 17B rue Gaston Boissier in Chaville-Viroflay, not far from the woods, where the lilies of the valley had an odor of war because the nearby airfield at Villacoublay was often bombarded.

So our family moved to Viroflay during the summer of 1943. We stayed in that lovely house until the Liberation. Mother searched for someone to whom to entrust her children during the dangerous trips to Paris, where she went indefatigably to continue to support her husband. Besides, she was officially registered in the Fifteenth Arrondissement. That was where she could pick up her rationing coupons. Fortunately there was Madame Aimée, our dear and faithful Madame Leprêtre, who lived in Chaville and who came afterwards to help Sophie Koulomzin.

They put me in kindergarten in the nearby Catholic school. I think I recall going there on foot, and the atmosphere of the place was sweet to my little girl's heart after being traumatized by the frightful boarding school at La Ferté-Allais. I came home with good marks. A photo shows me proudly displaying a medal. A shining memory comes back to me—one summer day when the white lilacs were blooming in the garden, I brought a big sweet-smelling bouquet to my dear teacher.

There were alerts followed by bombardments. One of them began as an adventure—the population of Chaville-Viroflay was invited to take shelter in the woods because they predicted an Allied bombardment. Together with Madame Aimée, we left on a picnic. The weather was nice and the forest had a lot of appeal. We came back carefree because no alert had happened. The bombardment came at night. The sky was streaked with flashes of lightning, and there were thunder and explosions everywhere. Just before dawn the garden was full of shell fragments. Another alert took us by surprise on a class day. We were going down into the basement quickly and the teachers started saying their rosary. "Hail Mary, full of grace, the Lord is with you . . ." my companions recited, frightened to death while the school was shaken by explosions. I knew my prayers in Russian, and I tried with all my strength to recite them against the current of those in French, but I didn't succeed. I, too, trembled with fear, distress, and vexation.

In the letters Mother wrote to Papa, she sent him photos of us and told him that I was praying fervently for his freedom. I don't remember it at all. On the other hand, I do remember that the evil that held my father in that distant image was called Hitler. It seems that I asked if Hitler would repent. That question moved Mother a great deal. According to all the evidence, she was pestered by the metaphysical problem of evil and the trial we were undergoing.

One day Mother went to Lourmel to clear out the room that another family was going to occupy. All her past came back to her. With her heart breaking, she tidied up the little room next to ours which had been used by Fr. Dimitri. "With death in my soul I had to upset everything that made up the spirit of that room, that still retained your warmth, your tenderness, all those little objects, a part of you . . ." she wrote to him.

Between the fifteenth and the eighteenth of September there occurred the one and only meeting between the Klepinin spouses. They were well prepared for it, but the meeting was difficult and sad. Mother had a hard time speaking about it even years afterward. "It was as if they had shown him to me and then taken him away, as if to shut me up. It was even harder than before." The meeting, in fact, was tragically short. When they parted, both of them had the impression that they had not said what was essential, so great was their emotion at seeing one another after seven months of separation.

Three months later the thing happened that they feared above everything else—the train to deport him. In his last letter Fr. Dimitri announced that he was going to leave for Germany. That fifteenth of December, 1943, 921 detainees were dispatched to Buchenwald. In a circular of April 21, 1942, that came from Berlin, the Nazi authorities had stipulated that "from now on the clergy will work like the others and can be assigned to all tasks."

# The Black Sun of the Summer of 1944 ෨

Ꮟ Mᴏᴛʜᴇʀ ᴡᴏᴜʟᴅ ʀᴇᴍᴀɪɴ ᴡɪᴛʜᴏᴜᴛ ɴᴇᴡs ꜰᴏʀ sᴇᴠᴇɴ months. It was only in June 1944 that she learned from her friends and companions in misfortune, Sophia Pianova and Judith Kazachkina, that Papa had died in February. Theodore Pianov, a detainee in Buchenwald, tried to make it clear to his wife—through letters that were examined closely by the German censors—that his friend Fr. Dimitri Klepinin was no longer. George Kazachkin saw him dying on February 9, and when he went back to visit him the next day, he learned that his body had been transferred to Buchenwald during the night—Dora did not yet have a crematorium. He, too, tried to write to his wife, "Dima is dead," but the SS guard tore up his letter and tossed the phrase at him, *"Bei uns stirbt man nicht"* ("Over here, people don't die"). In the following communication, which did not go out until the end of March and did not reach Judith until summer, George used the language of Aesop and wrote, "Tell Tamara that Dima has gone to join his mother." Theodore wrote something similar to his wife, who, with a broken heart, came to Chaville.

I still have a confused memory of that sunny day in June. There were people around Mother and she was crying. What do children do in situations like that? Having your mother in tears is too much to bear, and undoubtedly I must have cried as well, but more because of the general sadness. Seventeen months, in fact, separated me from the moment when for the last time I had my father alive. He had already turned into an abstraction, a myth, a ghost I would spend my whole life trying to conjure up, to sublimate, to learn to love beyond death and absence.

All his friends, his parishioners, the priests, and the metropolitan were overwhelmed. Metropolitan Eulogius organized a solemn funeral service at the cathedral. Not wanting to "tarnish the glorious name of Fr. Dimitri" by publishing an announcement card in the sole Russian journal, which was edited by the Fascist Zherebkov, he counted on word of mouth to spread the information. In fact, in spite of the absence of transportation in Paris on the eve of its liberation, the cathedral was jam-packed that day. Catherine Reitlinger described the ceremony in a letter to her sister Jeanne:[1] "When Vladyka had read the prayer of absolution by which the Church remits the sins of the departed, blessing him, accompanying him and letting him go to the other world, to the Lord, a current passed through the church, a sort of divine joy, luminous and solemn, as at Pascha. His widow was not an ordinary widow, either—without tears, collected, she was radiant, strong, herself 'paschal.' I have never before seen a widow like her. I thought—this is how Christians must say farewell to their brothers and those dear to them."

---

1   Undated manuscript letter. H.A.K. Archives.

# VII

## *Epilogue*

# The Liberation of Paris ✴

✴ PARIS WAS LIBERATED THE FOLLOWING MONTH. I WAS SIX years old, and we were at Chaville. I still have a very precise memory of that event. The evening before the American cars arrived at Versailles, Judith and Mother were occupied with sewing English and American flags. While the sewing machine was clicking, somebody rang the doorbell. Through the window Mother saw a German soldier in uniform. Panic all around! I saw Judith fold up the flags quickly, slip them under a cushion, and sit down on them. Mother went down to open the door and then came back upstairs, relieved—the soldier was retreating and only wanted a glass of water!

The next day, Madame Aimée, Judith, Mother, Paul, and I left by the Avenue de Versailles to go see the Allied troops arrive. The atmosphere was jubilant. A rather large crowd was rushing about on all sides. The women were wearing light dresses and had flowers in their arms. There was a fantastic rumbling of vehicles, and I was struck by their immense caterpillar tracks. The American soldiers threw us little green sticks of something, and I held in my hand my first piece of chewing gum. All of a sudden the column of cars stopped, some women perched on the sidewalk, and then an event took place which has been evoked for a long time as a subject for commentary in our family—Judith climbed up into a car in her turn and—oh!, what a surprise!—a huge black American gave her two big kisses on the cheek! Blushing with confusion, Judith jumped to the ground, and Mother and Madame Aimée teased her lightheartedly. They often reminded her of her "US flirt."

But then along came some Frenchmen in civilian clothes and arm-bands who made the crowd move back toward the adjacent streets. We were in danger, because the French Forces of the Interior were surrounding a house where some collaborators were hiding. We heard some shots. The adults took us in their arms and we quickly made it home again. From that point on, whenever we talked about the liberation of Paris, I would see those cars again, that black American, and that house at the end of a park, surrounded by armed men.

It is clear that these memories have been modified thanks to what has been evoked by adults during a good part of my life. But that's how we put together our lived experience, it seems to me. Memory is a reinvention. At the same time it is collective. It belongs to the family and even to the clan, and it can be equally shared with strangers who have lived through the same events in another way.

# The Time of Transmission 🙾

🙾 *T*HEN LIFE WENT BACK TO NORMAL. THE PRISONERS STARTED to return, so thin they could hardly be recognized. And so Pianov and Kazachkin showed up, the only members of Orthodox Action to escape. It was from them, on their return, that Mother finally learned when and how Fr. Dimitri died. She went to Metropolitan Eulogius on rue Daru. She was not able to go see Fr. Sergius Bulgakov, who was dying. In the circle around Fr. Sergius they told him that Fr. Dimitri had been liberated. His home nurses, wanting to cheer him up, had taken advantage of a remission to announce this false news to him. Fr. Sergius smiled and crossed himself.

George Kazachkin, my father's faithful friend and godfather of my little brother Paul, returned with an affliction of the lungs. He had to leave almost immediately for the sanatorium. Since the Buchenwald archives had been burned, his testimony was necessary to vouch for the death of Fr. Dimitri. After having taken many steps, Mother finally obtained a pension as a war widow. Our family record book was adorned with the statement that "Father died for France," thanks to which we received a national scholarship.

From that point on, every year—on the anniversary of Papa's death— we organized get-togethers at the house. A priest friend came to celebrate a requiem, and then the adults recounted their memories. I felt the sympathy they had for us. We lived very humbly. Some Jews who had escaped the pursuit and who lived in the United States sent us packages of food and clothing. They even invited my brother to Pennsylvania; he came back dazed and loaded down with gifts.

Mother took up her activities again at the YMCA. We also participated in the meetings of the RSCM. In particular we went out in the summer for the Saint-Theoffrey camp in the Isère region of the French Alps. I attended Protestant conferences in England and participated in the Fellowship of St. Alban and St. Sergius. Mother's vow came true—she had transmitted to us the "torch of mutual understanding between Christians." She had raised us in the memory of that heroic priest who had merely passed through our lives, and yet I felt that he was truly present.

From time to time she gave interviews to writers who were researching the attitude of Orthodox Christians during the Occupation. Alongside Geneviève de Gaulle and Elisabeth Behr-Sigel she participated in a television broadcast about Mother Maria and the Orthodox Action moderated by Fr. Jean Renneteau[1] at Noisy. Some Soviet journalists came to interview her. She had the pleasure of receiving Natalia Ruzhina, whom Fr. Dimitri had snatched from the claws of the Gestapo and who had told her that in her distant Moldova, her family venerated my father.

The joys and the triumphs of the Church were Mother's own. In that regard she was astonishingly modern, approving the emergence of services in French, the publication of bilingual catechisms, and the participation of laity in parish life. She never missed any of the RSCM conferences and took special pleasure when celebrities were invited, such as Abbé Pierre, Fr. Alexander Schmemann, or Olivier Clément.

Editorial assistant at the United Editors-YMCA Press publishing house, Mother invited us to share her joy at the publication of the first books of Solzhenitsyn, her pride at having published under her own name the excellent bibliography of the works of Nikolai Berdyaev, followed by a second volume dedicated to works about that Russian thinker she admired so much. She was always active and cheerful, and the physical pains of old age did not burden her. She applied to herself her famous formula: "In everything, keep the hierarchy of values." At the top of that hierarchy was the Spirit, the Paraclete.

She passed away on October 7, 1987, full of days.

---

1   Educated at the St. Sergius Institute, Fr. Jean Renneteau was responsible for the Orthodox broadcasts on French television before becoming, in 1974, priest of the French-speaking parish of St. Catherine in Geneva-Chambésy (Switzerland).

# Grandfather Andrey &ograve;&eacute;

&ograve;&eacute; *A*T THE BEGINNING OF THIS ESSAY, I EVOKED THE FIGURE OF my grandmother, who played such a determining role in Fr. Dimitri's spiritual evolution. Now I would like to say a few words about my grandfather Andrey, the architect.

He was a gentle and humble man. I got to know him in 1952, two years before he died, when he came to live in France with his daughter Tatiana. He never spoke to us about the buildings he designed, whether in Russia or in Serbia, and as a result we never suspected what a great architect he had been. It was only after his death that I discovered the grandiose establishment of the Narzan Baths in Kislovodsk, which he had erected between 1901 and 1903 in the style of the palaces of Razhahstan, with an elegant staircase. My children and I were proud to see the plaque bearing his name on that prestigious palace. Later I saw the two buildings he constructed in Odessa, which are also considered to be historical monuments. In Belgrade he built the church that served the Russian colony of the Yugoslavian capital. I regret the fact that I didn't question him about the childhood of his children and their life in Russia.

Nevertheless I have a letter from him in which he recounts a mystical experience that is linked to the death of his son Dmitri:

It was the autumn of 1944. I was in the hospital in Bor, a lonely old man of seventy-two years old. I had just learned that my son had died in Germany. It's easy to figure my state of mind. Fortunately I had no resentment toward those who had caused the death of my son. That allowed me to bear my cross more easily. I can't honestly say I had forgiven my "debtors," but, let me repeat, I didn't have any resentments.

We regret the death of those who are close to us and we weep for them, but to tell the truth, it's really ourselves that we mourn. The belief in another world must inspire us so that—if we are sure that the life of the dear one is such that it does not allow any doubt to hover over us with regard to his salvation and the Lord's gift of eternal life—we should not weep but rejoice. All the same we are weak and without the aid of the Most High we cannot resolve ourselves to accept our fate.

Here you see what a state I was in. My illness had passed, I went out for a walk every day, and I was supposed to leave the hospital before long. One of the last mornings I was lying on my bed. I don't remember what I was thinking about, but I am sure that I was in a completely normal state physically and psychologically. Now suddenly an extraordinary phenomenon happened in me—it was if I were turned into two people. My eyes saw clearly the ill people in the room, the familiar landscape out the window, whereas the interior of the room was illuminated by an intense light such as does not exist on earth. It was not the sun or electricity, or any other earthly light.

Even the mind of a skeptic could not claim that all that was imaginary or that I had invented it. How, in fact, could I have imagined something that did not exist, which could not be described in human words? Certainly—given how little faith we have in miracles—we would end up finding a human explanation for what happened to me if, by chance, it were not for the most important thing—that in that instant I perceived clearly the existence of the soul, and I felt a happiness and joy that cannot be expressed in any human words.

I am quite familiar with human happiness and joy. God, in His indulgence, has given me a lot of them in the course of my life. I know the miracle of healing (respected doctors had said that I would remain hunchbacked) and I have twice escaped death from a terrible wound. I have known joy and happiness in my family life, the joy of success in my work and my creativity, as well as a total sense of well-being. All that can be recounted and understood. But what I lived through at that moment does not allow itself to be grasped by the reason. It is what Christ calls "perfect joy."

A skeptical mind will pose the question of knowing whether an ordinary sinful man can be worthy of such happiness, of such a miracle. But to this question as well Christ replies, "It is the sick and not the healthy who have need of a physician." Or again, "Can an old father who weeps over the death of his son reach the point of being so happy?"

As I reread these lines I cannot help thinking that Fr. Dimitri had received from God, several months after his glorious end, the grace to visit his aged father and to console him.

# *This Saint Lived Among Us* ဆ

ဆ $A$S IF WITH A SORT OF PREMONITION, HIS MOTHER HAD grasped his little child's hand as he was dying and blessed the members of his family who were gathered around his cradle. Anna, his aunt, remembered that benediction when he was newly ordained a priest and came out of the sanctuary of the St. Alexander Nevsky Cathedral to bless the faithful. That hand had then consecrated the holy gifts, been placed on the head of penitents, blessed his parishioners, made the sign of the cross over the departed, and traced over the body of the baptized the seal of the gift of the Holy Spirit. Before the officer of the Gestapo, that hand had pointed to the Crucified Lord on his pectoral cross—"And this Jew here, do you know Him?"

On a walk one day with Fr. Basil Zenkovsky, Fr. Dimitri told him, "A priest's hands do not belong to him." Several minutes before he died, Fr. Dimitri needed another man to take his hand and make the sign of the cross over him.

Today this humble deportee and glorious martyr has become a saint. The Orthodox Church, acting through the Ecumenical Patriarch of Constantinople, inscribed him on the list of innumerable witnesses of Christ who intercede for us on January 16, 2004. By doing this the Church has brought the very idea of sainthood closer to us. Each of us is called to sainthood, each of us receives a powerful encouragement to lead a life in the perspective of the building of the Kingdom.

Saint Dimitri, so close to us, so present among us, raise your hand and bless us!

*July 20, 2004*
*Feast of the Synaxis of Saints Alexis, Dimitri, Maria, George[1], and Elias*

---

1   Yuri Skobtsov (Georgii is the Slavonic form of Yuri).

# ❧ VIII ❧

# *Letters from Prison Camp*

# I
## Compiègne, March 23, 1943

*My own beloved Tomik,*

*Christ be with you and the little ones! Thank you for the two packages of food and the suitcase with the liturgical items. I pray that God will protect my little birds. I am constantly with you in thought, especially at 11 PM, when the forty-eight men of our barracks are asleep. [. . .] I am waiting for the antimension and the vessels. We do not have a church, but we will be able to celebrate in the quarters for the Catholic priests, with whom we get along well. Fr. Dimitri Sobolev lives with them.*

*At first the trial was hard and I was worried about you. But after I received the package of March 21, my life changed completely. Don't worry about the future. Give yourself up completely to the will of God. His solicitude and love prevent me from having any fear or any concern about the future. It is clear that we had to pass through everything that happened and this will serve both for my good and for everyone's, in spite of all the difficulty of your situation. I pray that God will preserve you from worry on my behalf. When I come back, we will live joyfully and cheerfully. Little Paul will have learned to walk and will then have not merely two, but all his teeth.*

*The time here does not pass idly. We study Prat. We read him out loud, either sitting on my bed or outside on the lawn. Everyone is in good shape. I hope that I will not be separated from Yuri Skobstov. It's in his interest, because I think I will be useful to him. He looks healthy.*

*What is painful is the crowding and the overpopulation. But we are struggling to maintain a rule for our life. We gather for prayer in the evening and the morning. Keifer[1] and Anatoly[2] join us from the room next door. I think*

---

1   Nickname given to George Kazachkin.
2   Anatoly Viskovsky, handyman of the house on Lourmel Street, had been freed from a psychiatric asylum by Mother Maria.

*back nostalgically to Romainville. Life with Fr. Mikhail Belsky was well ordered there. We lived in a separate room and we could pray and celebrate the services, which Mother Maria attended. We felt geographically close to you. I was over-whelmed by your thermos of hot coffee that retained the warmth of our house. I was stirred by the thought that my dear Tomik had been quite close to me, since I guessed that she had brought this coffee. Receiving parcels from you is a great event, especially to recognize the familiar handwriting and know that every-thing is going well. It would have been the height of blessedness to remain near you all.*

*May the Lord, the Mother of God, and all the saints preserve you.*
*Your Sobaka.*

## 2
## April 11, 1943

*My own beloved Tomik,*

*As of yesterday we have been separated for two months. How are my little birds? Let's think more about the joy of reunion than the pain of separation. I see clearly the advantage of the trial that has been sent to us—to see the vanity of all plans and calculations and submit entirely to the divine will. Previously I had put too much trust in the fact that God's love was manifest in exterior well-being. Now I discover His care in trials. Be cheerful, joyful, and partake often of the holy gifts.*

*Tomorrow we are going to drop off our requests for packages. There are fif-teen Russians here. On Annunciation we celebrated matins in the room of the Catholic priests. On the same day I received your wonderful package. We pray for everyone who helps us. Thanks to the packages, we do not suffer from hun-ger and we share with those who do not have anything, in particular with two Poles, our neighbors from Romainville. [. . .] There are three Serbs who receive very skimpy packages. One of them will need some help, he's dying of hunger. Perhaps from the church's funds you could send him some biscuits like the ones we used to send to Tourelle.[3] I am touched by how thoughtful my wise Tomkin is with the packages.*

*When I return, Pavkin will have all his teeth. How has Ladik gotten used to living with Sonia?[4] Thank her. When the weather is nice, we sit outside on the*

3   Tourelle is one of the camps where the committee of Orthodox Action sent pack-
    ages to Russians who were confined there.
4   Sophie Koulomzin.

*lawn, read, pray, and study Prat. Please send me the Summa Catholica. When the racket of the forty-eight occupants of the barracks dies down toward eleven o'clock, I pray and think of you, my little puppies. I pray for all my friends. Yuri is in good condition, both physically and morally. Keifer is with us. They have just cut off the heat, but we manage all the same to warm our supper of the things in the packages.*

*Read 2 Timothy 2:3–7 and 3:12, as well as James 1:2–3. This corresponds to everything we are living through. I try to imagine everything in your life. I have no concerns on the material plane, knowing that decent people are not going to leave my birds in distress. I would love to know whether you see people and whether you manage to have a little break, to laugh and relax. Don't worry on my account. We are all in good shape. Go and see Smetankin's wife. She needs some financial help. Thank God that the Church exists! I give a big kiss to Fr. Basil Zenkovsky and the members of the choir. I long to see them.*

*It concerns me that you have not moved to another apartment.[5] Do it as soon as you can. When you are there you will be able to wait for Sobaka to return and we will build an active and interesting life. Kiss Zhenya[6] (how is she?) and also Babushka[7] and everybody else.*

*Christ is with you, my loves. I give you a big embrace.*

*Sobaka.*

*P.S.: If possible, send me the cross and the icon that were brought to the church to be blessed. The chanter knows where to find them.*

*Other than the Serbs, some packages from the Red Cross would be welcome for George Klubov (10705) and Nikolai Zhdanovsky (10327), who are very thin. Thank you for the tobacco, it cheers me greatly. I smoke seldom, when I am alone in my bunk in the evening.*

[Note from Yuri Skobtsov in French, added to this letter.]
*My dear friends,*

*Our good spirits depend on yours. Write Mother that I am doing well and that all I think about is you. I give a tender embrace to my little grandmother, Dad, and Jean,[8] as well as O. M.*

---

5   Lourmel was often under surveillance by the Germans, and his wife was not secure there.
6   Zhenya is Evgenia Patzer, a very close friend whose problems Fr. Dimitri had taken to heart.
7   Babushka is the grandmother of Yuri Skobstov, Sophia Pilenko.
8   This refers to his friend Jean Loth, about whom we know nothing.

*I am touched by your concerns, but you must not deprive yourselves. May God protect you. Be happy. Send your photos in a package. It is to you, Jean, that I entrust Grandmother. I have confidence in you and I am proud of you.*

## 3
## May 2, 1943

*Christis risen![9]*
*My dear Tomik,*

*Glory to God, they have not yet sent us away. In the meantime there was a new transport and Mother Maria left on it. She passed through here one evening and stayed until the following morning. Yuri met her.*

*We celebrate liturgy every day. That changes everything because as you said, we feel our liturgical communion with you. Thank you for the packages, my Tomik. Our family has grown by three Russian young men.*

*My dear Tomik, how much I have to tell you! The most important change in our life is the services. I am at peace concerning what the divine will has in store for us, but I feel even more acutely the desire to go back home. Separation weighs heavily on me. But I keep my spirits up. I am focusing less on the necessity of the trial and more on the need to begin pastoral work, because the number of Russians is growing. At first I was preoccupied solely with keeping up my own morale. I have read both volumes of Prat, and now I'm reading the Bible with the commentary of Fillion. I associate mostly with Yuri, who is in good shape physically and spiritually. Tell that to his grandmother.*

*It is 10:30 PM, the Frenchmen are in bed, and it's the most blessed hour. We sit around the table, writing and reading. I have the upper bunk next to the window, above Anatoly. Fr. Dimitri is in the neighboring bunk above Yuri. Across from me is Fyodor Timofeyevich. Keifer is two beds away so that we form a Russian corner, eleven of us Russians in the room.*

*When the day is over, I climb onto my bed, smoke a cigarette and think about my little puppies. Then I pray for them and soon go to sleep. In the morning we get up at 7:00 AM, put some tea into a thermos, and go to roll call, which lasts from thirty minutes to an hour. Then I read the epistles of St. Paul or the precommunion prayers. Then I celebrate liturgy, followed by tea with those who have received communion—usually Fr. Dimitri, Yuri, and I. Then I read on my bunk. Sometimes I manage to sleep a little after breakfast. During the day the uproar is so terrible that we lose track of time somehow; time gets away from me.*

9 Pascha fell on April 25 that year.

*I meet with people or read. In the afternoon, at 5:30 PM, there is roll call again, then vespers and supper prepared with food from the packages, cocoa or tea. Afterwards, we have conversation. Tomorrow, Sunday, we are going to have a feast with the Pascha packages. We did not receive them in time for Pascha. I am waiting impatiently for the news of your moving to a new place. I think it's very important, because otherwise I am worried about my little birds.*

*On my birthday[10]—for the first time since I was captured—I drank a glass of vodka. I was on my bed, and a man I barely knew happened to receive a package, and came over and offered it to me. I thought perhaps my Tomkin was just then spending an evening with our friends and toasting my health. In this way the Lord arranged that I could join you. Large things are revealed in the small, even in details like that. This little glass warmed my heart.*

*I am so glad that everything is going well in the church. We mention the parishioners every day in our prayers.*

*Now I have some requests. Some copies of the New Testament and some prayerbooks to distribute (thank you for the icons!), a box for the incense, a tabernacle for the holy gifts, without utensils. We have prepared a reserve supply of the holy gifts.*

*Thank you, my Tomik, for all these tasks carried out with love. I embrace my little birds and bless them. Christ be with you.*

*Your loving*

*Dimsky*

*P.S.: Ask Vladyka if, in case of my liberation, he authorizes me to leave my antimension to Fr. Sobolev so as not to deprive the Russians and the other Orthodox of the liturgy.*

*P.S. 2: Did you write my father that I am a prisoner? Do you have news of him?[11]*

## 4
## May 9, 1943
## Feast of the Myrrh-Bearers

*My dear Tomik,*

*I congratulate you on your feast day, which we celebrated today. Don't be discouraged or weak. You support me by your courage. After all, there is nothing*

10  April 14.
11  Andrey Klepinin worked during the war as an architect in Belgrade.

*tragic. It's not going to last forever. Consider our separation not as our being torn apart, but as my being sent by the Church on a missionary journey for several months. And in fact that is pretty much the way it is—I celebrate, preach, hear confessions, and so forth. At the worst, they will send me to work in Germany, but as you see there have been four convoys and we have all escaped. Perhaps we will have that good fortune. And even in Germany there won't be anything terrible. We will no doubt have more freedom as workers. The important thing is the evidence of divine solicitude toward us which protects us everywhere. But do everything you can to leave Lourmel. You are the one who sees what you need to undertake, but I am not at ease knowing that you are there, although on the other hand you are under the protection of the Mother of God, the Church, and the sacraments. You decide, my Tomik.*

*We celebrate liturgy every day, sometimes in one little room and sometimes in another. The Red Cross took my bag that contained the liturgical vessels. I will ask for it back when their representative comes.*

*Be joyful, my beloved Tomik. This trial was necessary for us. I was always afraid that we relied too much on material well-being. We will come out of this trial as more seasoned troops. It is time for roll call.*

*Greet our friends, and also Babadzhan.*

*Dima who loves you very much.*

[Note from Yuri in red pencil:]
*May Christ watch over you. I embrace you. Yuri.*

## 5
## May 19, [1943]

*My dear Tomik,*

*I have just ten minutes to write. Thank God, morale is improving. I just received three hundred francs and this very day two packages came. The shoes are very nice, I will wear them for a long time. Thank the people who donated them. For the moment there is no longer a question of leaving. On the contrary, it seems we are putting down roots here. Today they made us clean the barracks. They promised that we would have the right to two postcards a month. We often think about the work our packages cause you. Pianov is getting ready to put in a request to be liberated.*

*I must not be dissociated from Orthodox Action. We bear all the responsibility and at the same time, we are not guilty of anything.*

*Christ be with you, my dear birds. I embrace you.*
*Dima.*

[Note from George Kazachkin to his wife:]
*Dear Iudinka!*
    *I received your note. I am very happy for you. Please don't worry about me.*
*I received the paper. Your packages are wonderful. Did you receive the ring? I*
*will write to you the first chance I get. For the moment I am pressed for time. I*
*embrace you. I congratulate you and in my thoughts I send you-know-what.*
    *Your Yuri who loves you.*

# 6
## June 2, 1943
## Eve of the Ascension

*My beloved dear Tomik,*
    *I congratulate you and Pavkin as well as Ladik on her feast day.*[12] *Tell her*
*that I think about her and pray for her all the time. God be praised that you have*
*recovered your good spirits. We have to be patient with the idea that our separa-*
*tion may be long and not delude ourselves with illusions about liberation in the*
*near future. Otherwise time is going to drag even more slowly. When all is said*
*and done this cannot last forever. But on the other hand, what joy awaits us! We*
*have counted too much on exterior well-being (that is, on escaping from danger).*
*When we have our family life back again, we will be seasoned in patience.*
    *We have some changes. Fr. Dimitri, Yuri, and I now have our own separate*
*quarters as members of the clergy. This room serves for a church, and we cele-*
*brate liturgy there every day. Our barrack, near the previous ones, has few peo-*
*ple in it—just three little rooms for administration, the three Catholic clerics and*
*us. From now on we will be able to study, pray, and enjoy the silence. I conduct*
*a study circle on the Gospels using Prat.*
    *We continue to have supper with our friends in the neighboring barracks. At*
*9 o'clock, when people can no longer walk around the camp, we feel like we are*
*in a monastery. The silence is absolute. The windows look out over the square.*
*In front of us are grass, trees, and a clear view. God is merciful. If only I could*
*use the circumstances to be useful. The members of our circle are Fr. Dimitri,*

---

12  June 3 on the Julian calendar (liturgical date May 21) is the feast day of Ss. Constan-
    tine and Helen.

*Pianov, Kazachkin, and Yuri. My nerves are starting to calm down after all the racket, the swearing and the fights over the food. I am certainly ashamed in front of those who remain down there, but I console myself by thinking that I will be better able to serve them.*

*How I would love to have a more detailed glimpse of your life! I don't stop making plans for our future life. How beautiful it will be! I think that my neurasthenia, brought on by constantly feeling that I could not fulfill my pastoral duties, will fade considerably, thanks to that interruption in which they are reduced to practically zero. Thus there is no evil without some good, provided only that my birds are living through this time without difficulty. It would be a good thing if you could move somewhere right away—make some kind of change in your circumstances.*

*When you take steps to help me, do not under any circumstances dissociate me from Orthodox Action. That would cast a shadow on them. It would be like agreeing with the accusations.*

*Tomorrow we are getting ready to celebrate Ladik's feast day. Leonty Klimov moved me with his flowers plucked from I don't know where. In our room after our studies, we will gather for tea. [. . .]*

*Good night, my beloved Tomik. Tomorrow, on Ladik's feast, I will pray in particular for you and in the morning I will write more about what came to me during the night.*

*I give you a big hug, very tight, my tenderly beloved, courageous puppies. Write in detail about Pavkin. How is he showing his personality? Your photos are hanging above my bed. It was a great joy to receive them, just as when I received the photo of Pavkin when I was in Romainville. On Ascension we will say a moleben for Ladik's health and have some tea. I give a big hug to my birds.*

7

### July 1, [1943]

*I received the package of vestments. Thank you, Tomkin. You remembered everything Sobaka needed. I celebrated getting the tobacco, and all the other things, above all the rubber insoles and the sandals, because my feet were too warm. The sandals will serve to preserve my shoes for the winter.*

*Today I received the package for the church. The small-sized prosphora are welcome. I will force myself to empty the bottles. Where did you get those bottles? In the next package, try to send the two small Bibles that are stored in Pianov's study and an additional four Gospels, but only if it isn't too difficult to get them.*

*I'm afraid I am complicating your task and I imagine what a problem it must be to put together our packages.*

*You will soon receive the power of attorney. A few days ago, in fact, I was summoned to the camp commander for fingerprints. The power of attorney was transmitted as well as a request to the camp commander—I asked him to grant me a visit to settle my affairs with the apartment and my family.*

*Popov and many others have been liberated. It's useless, therefore, to send them anything. It would be good to send a package to Makarov (No. 13407) because he doesn't receive anything from anybody. He has been with us since Romainville. There has been a rumor since Pascha that the camp might be completely transferred to some indeterminate location in France. I need to know what address for you to write in case it becomes impossible to transmit letters.*

*The photo of Pavkin gave me great joy. He is someone completely new to me, a well-asserted personality. Ladkin has not changed a lot. The photos are a great joy. Write me the details about the life of my birds. Ladkin is certainly rendering little services and taking Pavkin under her supervision.*

*I am enthusiastically occupying myself with the choir, composed of five or six persons. I am little by little learning to give the pitch. For that it's necessary for the next chant already to be resonating in my head and then it begins to come. Sometimes we quarrel. The chanters get upset and stop chanting and then they end up coming back together. Fortunately Yuri is very devoted to the Church. He is preparing for the priesthood (it's a secret). For him, it is a well-settled desire. It is hard to figure out when and how it will happen. From now on, my course in the New Testament will not happen twice a week but only once. Fr. Andrey[13] will offer a course in liturgics. That is fine with me, because I will be able to prepare without hurrying, use more documentation and, in addition to the Gospel, I can deal with St. Paul. The Catholics have a copy of Prat on St. Paul.*

*The chanting draws those among us Russians who do not often go to church because they like to be more active. That's exactly what Klubov and his friend Zhdanovsky felt. Our church is very nice. Here is more or less what it looks like (drawing). The iconostasis is made of some beds with tables arranged against them. On the altar are the holy gifts. Fr. Andrey offered us some liturgical objects but the beauty of our chapel comes from what my Tomkin—so full of wisdom—sent us.*

*On Sundays we celebrate in turn. From now on I am resolved not to celebrate on Sunday because the chanting suffers. Now on Sundays we enjoy having*

13   Fr. Andrey Galkin-Vrassky.

*good chanting. Starting with this Sunday, I am going to celebrate a morning lit-urgy at 6:00 AM, with just Yuri, because nobody has permission to walk around in the camp before 7:00 AM. For Yuri and me this will be a form of communion with you and the whole parish of the Protection of the Mother of God.*

*Tell Ladkin that I did this drawing for her so that she will know in what church her papa is celebrating liturgy.*

*I am happily wearing the sandals. The lighter is very useful to me, because they confiscated our gasoline and we do not have any matches. If you can, send me some wicks.*

*Give Tanya and Zhenya a big hug and congratulate Fr. Sergius[14] on my behalf.*

*Greet our friends. I thank all those who help you and who help us. If one of our friends could give his tobacco, for example Volodya, this would be beneficial, because smoking keeps up the morale and besides, we trade tobacco for food. Thanks, Tomik, for the medicine. I will be able to take care of myself. Take cour-age, my Tomik, every passing day brings the time closer that we will be together again. The war is not going to last forever and we will see one another again soon. Tell Tanya that we will see one another again soon. Write me how you are living in the countryside and whether there are letters from my father. How do you sort it out to do everything you are doing? Aren't you getting overly tired? Don't be afraid to spend a little money in order to save your strength. Ask our friends for some money in my name. May God watch over you, my dearly be-loved Tomik. Every evening I go to the church to pray for you and I bless you with the altar cross.*

*I embrace all the members of the choir, I greet all the monks and nuns and all our friends, the Marchenkos.[15] How is Zhenya?*

*One more time, I embrace you.*

*Your Dimsky.*

*P.S.: I am not afraid of anything except compromises that lack divine grace. Tell me about the situation of the Church.*

*Don't worry about me. I am not hiding anything from you.*

---

14  Fr. Sergius Bulgakov celebrated the twenty-fifth anniversary of his priesthood on the Monday of Pentecost, 1943.

15  It is doubtless by secret agreement that Mark and Stella Romanchenko, friends of the Klepinins, are designated in this way. Stella was baptized by Fr. Dimitri, and Tamara was her godmother.

## 8
## July 8, 1943

*My dearly beloved Tomik,*

*I am responding to your letter from yesterday. My previous letter has not gone out yet. They brought it back to me because they didn't find anyone to pass it through. I am sitting in the sanctuary of our chapel, and it's 6:30 AM. Yesterday evening we didn't have any light and I couldn't write to you. You mustn't worry about me. I describe to you everything I am living through without hiding anything. The hardest thing is to be separated from you. Everything else will do me good. I don't think our health suffers from lack of food thanks to the packages. Right now the soup at noon is quite a bit better. They distribute commodities to us more often, such as cheese, sausage, and butter. But what saves us from starving is certainly the packages.*

*I don't keep anything for myself, Tomik, because you see, the four of us put everything into a common pot. Also apart from a few personal delicacies such as chocolate, we share everything and no one loses anything. The only one who is in debt to us is Fr. Dimitri Sobolev who, for all practical purposes, doesn't receive any packages. I think when they start sending packages to Fr. Andrey we will be in the midst of abundance because he will receive something for the different people who share with him. Apart from this sharing, the rest of the packages go to prepare the evening soup.*

*Tomik, in spite of your instructions I wrote to the address of Vas[16] because we missed the possibility of having that letter pass through the usual way. I think the packages intended for the church and addressed to Fr. Andrey will not meet any obstacle, because they tolerate them here. Tomik, in July I have the right to two packages, but I am afraid that by the time this letter arrives the month will be over. We have a big shortage of tobacco.*

*I dream that when I am liberated I will have a feast with Tomkin. You will make me a suit like a layman. I'll take you to the movies and then we'll go and sit in a café somewhere on the Champs-Elysées with a cigarette and watch the crowd pass by . . . I don't think a dream like that is a reaction to the monotony of our lives, but first of all the sign of a better frame of mind; and secondly, I want you to enjoy a happier life than at Lourmel. Lourmel was a somber place, as you recall—a mixture of Dostoyevsky and Zoshchenko.[17] It's possible that the*

16  This refers to Professor Basil Zenkovsky.
17  Mikhail Zoshchenko is a satiric author who often depicts the harsh reality of the Soviet communal apartments.

*Lord will send us an even more difficult period of life, but at Lourmel, there was plenty of pointless agitation. Tell me about the parish's financial situation—has it gone completely out of Babushka's control? [. . .]*

*I must close, Tomkin, and begin the proskomedia,[18] and then there will be the whistle for roll call, after which the liturgy will continue. I am happy that the preparation of packages does not weigh too heavily on you. Thank you, my good Tomik, I feel that you prepare each object with love, and you never forget your Sobaka's smallest request. I ask again that you request tobacco from the people who are better off. For us it is a moral support and it kills our appetite. Even though there is no famine, we are still hungry after every meal, and a cigarette alleviates that sensation.*

*I give you a big hug. May Christ be with you, my birds.*
*Dima.*


*P.S.: I am taking the medicine, which is starting to have an effect. I've felt much better the last few days.*


## 9
## July 18, 1943
## Feast of St. Sergius


*My dearly beloved Tomik,*
*The Lord continues to watch over us in all things. How are my birds? How did your move to the country work out? I often think that all these movings-out and movings-in must not be easy for Tomik without Sobaka's help, although I am sure that your friends help you. When will the time come that our little nest will be gathered again under the same roof?*

*All the same, not for a minute must we forget that this trial is God's infinite mercy, the fruits of which could not be appreciated under other circumstances. It is the pledge of an even greater happiness, I am sure. In what concerns me personally, one of the positive sides of my stay here is that I have been partially freed of neurasthenia in my activities. Sometimes the feeling that I haven't done this or that or that I have to run somewhere comes back, but that happens less and less often. In order to achieve this, it has been necessary for me to live through an experience in which there is no longer any question of running about. May the*

---

18  Office of preparation of the offerings (holy gifts) intended for the eucharistic sac-
    rifice in the Orthodox liturgy.

*Lord allow me, on my return to activity, to keep my calm and my confidence in myself (in the good sense of the term). And above all, may this trial not leave you with your nerves broken. Do as much as you can to save your strength, and do not be afraid to spend money. Ask for it in my name. "If we have sown spiritual things for you, is it a great thing if we reap your material things?" (1 Corinthians 9:11).*

*Here is how my day goes—I get up at 5:45 or 6:00 AM and go to the church and prepare for communion (once or twice a week I don't receive communion, but study instead). If I celebrate, I complete the proskomedia as quickly as possible. I have drawn up a new list of the living and the dead which is pretty complete. Then I take off my vestments and go to roll call, which lasts around half an hour. We line up in rows according to our barracks. Then I return to the church where, at 8:30 AM, the liturgy begins. On Sundays I always celebrate a morning liturgy with Yuri, in which we pray especially for our parish. Towards 7:00 AM there resounds "Blessed is the kingdom*[19] *. . ." and we hurry to the second liturgy with the choir. In the choir are Fyodor Timofeyevich, Keifer, Fr. Dimitri Sobolev, and two other Russians, one of whom is a former seminarian. Our chanting is quite acceptable, and I am gradually learning to give the pitch. On Sundays the roll call takes place at 10:00 AM. I study theology with Yuri, who is more and more eager to enter the priesthood. I have prepared a series of talks on the historical context of the time of Christ, and afterwards we are continuing to study the commentary on the Gospel.*

*If Mother Maria does not return from captivity at the same time we do, we will have to take good care of Yuri.*

*Tomik, my dear, don't allow yourself to get discouraged. We will see one another again soon. God will arrange everything in the depth of His wisdom. As the trial is, so shall be the deliverance. Above all, let's keep our spirits up and walk on a straight path, in which is a blessing.*

*The book of the liturgy of St. John Chrysostom is in the sanctuary. Ask the reader to get it. We need candles and incense. Ask someone for an old winter cassock, because the ones I have are in tatters. I will send them back to you. For this summer, I am well provided. I have repaired my shoes, thanks to the diligence of my Tomik.*

*Give Ladkin and Pavlik a big hug. What new words does he know how to say? I embrace the Marchenkos, Zhenya, Tanya,*[20] *and all their family. My dear*

---

19  The doxology which opens the divine liturgy.
20  Tanya or Tatiana is Fr. Dimitri's sister.

*Tomik, may God watch over you, you and the children. I embrace you tenderly. Be joyful and cheerful.*

*Your Sobaka.*

## 10
## July 31, 1943

*My dearly beloved Tomik,*

*I received your letter of July 22. I am happy that the children are in the countryside for the dog-days. But why are you staying in town? Thank God here is news from my father. Write to him as you judge best and give him a big hug for me. Tell him that he absolutely must come and live with us after the war. Financial problems must not stand in the way of his living with us and his grandchildren. [. . .]*

*We have come to a good understanding, Yuri and I, with Fr. Andrey. He is a direct man who follows a determined path. That earns him a lot of enmity from many people and arouses a lot of rumors. As for me, I place complete confidence in him. On the contrary, the presence of Fr. Dimitri is a trial that was no doubt sent to us on purpose so that we might learn always to find a spiritual solution to difficulties. Up till now we have not had much success with this.*

*Three bombs were dropped by an airplane today in the American sector of the camp. Two of them did not explode and there were no victims. Our window looks right onto the place where they fell, two hundred meters away. The sound of the engines woke me, because the plane was flying at a low altitude. The explosion was deafening but it didn't do anything to our barracks. In the American camp, the visitors' block was half destroyed. This type of event is much less serious among us than in the city because the buildings are low and there is a lot of empty space for bombs to land.*

*We have some changes with the chapel. We lost the place where we were by ourselves, and we had to move to another place in the same barracks, to a room we share with the Protestants. Basically the only change is that we have to agree on the hours for services in the evening and I cannot be all by myself when I want, but that is not serious. If the Lord helps us to find the right approach with Fr. Dimitri and if they don't send us to Germany, everything will go well. They aren't talking about it for the moment, but since there is an influx of detainees we can expect people to leave.*

*I finished my course on the Old Testament today with the Prophets. I will come back on Monday for a talk about the Gospels. Today or tomorrow I am going to recopy the canon of pre-communion prayers for my personal use, intro-ducing the following modifications—in place of the irmi,[21] which are not inspir-ing to me, I read extracts from chapter six of the Gospel according to John on the Eucharist, which I have divided into eight complete phrases. Seeing that we have only one prayer book, it is more convenient for me to have my own canon and pray by myself. I am going to recopy it and glue it in the back of my Bible. Here, my Tomik, are the details of Sobaka's activities.*

*I am trying to picture to myself what Pavlik looks like at the age he is now. I am happy that Ladik now has a playmate. [. . .] Yuri gives me so much satis-faction. He has matured and become less emotional, less nervous. Spiritually, it seems to me he is treading a level, peaceful path. I am trying to transmit to him what I learned from Fr. Chetverikov.*

*I have a great appreciation for Fyodor Timofeyevich. He is an upright man and a true friend. In general we are forming a united family with Keifer and Fr. Andrey. The jarring note comes from Fr. Sobolev, who weighs everybody down although basically he's not a bad man. You, too, Tomik, say a prayer for us to be at our best and not react too humanly to his weaknesses, thereby wronging both him and ourselves.*

*May Christ be with you, my Tomik. I will continue my letter tomorrow. I have kept open the possibility of going to church early in the morning to recite my prayers and study. I also study between 9:00 and 10:00 PM, whereas during the day I study in the presence of others. But in comparison with Barracks A3, we are terribly privileged.*

*I embrace all our friends—Tanya, Zhenya, the choir, Marchenko. When will we at last be together? Let us be cheerful, remembering that all this is very nec-essary. The time will pass and joy will come. Thank Vladyka for the liturgical package.*

## II
## August 1, [1943]

*Some commissions. To the list of Russians, I am adding Avenir Vasiliev (No. 16364) and, if possible, a non-Russian, our parishioner from here, a very un-fortunate Greek, Kyriakidis (No. 9467), who asks that someone try to contact his family with whom he has lost contact since his arrest. Their address is 17 rue des Bannières in Marseilles. Entrust it to someone to contact a priest from Marseilles.*

21 Form of poetic liturgical chant.

*Dear Tomik, I'm sorry for flooding you with commissions. I received your package. Thank you. Everything is intact. The tobacco and the cigarettes are welcome. Thank those who contributed. In the future, add a little to the quantity of products for the soup. Perhaps you can ask Danilo Yermolayevich.[22] It so happens that for this month I am in debt for the cooking, even though in previous months my packages improved the common soup.*

*My dear Tomik, I will be with you in my prayers on August 3, although I cannot manage to remember what event is tied to that date. Write me news of the Church and give me details about your worries concerning our parish. I cannot believe that they have introduced fixed prices for the offices on demand! Concerning the list of the departed in January, I don't remember any longer, I have nothing on me. Perhaps you will find something among the papers I left at the house.*

*Go along then, my little one, my dearly beloved Tomik. May God watch over you and the children. I give you an embrace, as tight as I can. Thank and greet the servants of God Evgenia, Fr. Mikhail Chertkov, Fr. Cyprian and everyone else.*

*I thank Vladyka for the ecclesiastical packages.*

## 12
## August 15, [1943]

*My dearly beloved Tomik,*

*After the visit from S.A.[23] I learned that you had undergone a great deal more than I had known about. Always write me everything without hiding anything of your situation. In turn, I want you to have an exact picture of my life so that you will be completely reassured. The harshest trial was our arrival at Compiègne. We had no news, there were rumors that Paris had been bombarded, and we were afraid that you were worried. The food was very meager, just watery soup with pieces of rutabaga and two hundred grams of bread. In the morning, tea with sugar and in the evening tea without sugar, but we didn't have time to waste away from hunger because we had some things left over from Romainville. And then your packages began to arrive and were received with joy, along with the news that you were safe. You saved us from starvation. In barracks A3 we felt like bourgeois when we began to prepare soups with potato peels and chunks of lard.*

22 This refers to Danilo Skobtsov, Yuri's father and the ex-husband of Mother Maria.
23 This may refer to Sophia Alexeyevna Pianova.

*Today we have left the peelings behind. The standard-issue food is better—a thick soup with potatoes and often with pieces of meat. From time to time we get soup from the Red Cross. Every week they give out butter, preserves, and sausage. Lately, like today, they have sometimes even given us half a liter of wine.*

*In our barracks A2, we are completely cut off from the trial our people in A3 still have to endure—life in a common room. Our barracks is beginning to fill up, however (the only empty space is the chapel which we share with the Protestants), but the general commotion does not reach us. We are on a friendly and equal footing with the head men of the barracks, two Frenchmen who speak Russian. This is mostly thanks to Fr. Andrey, who knew how to make himself needed. The young people who distribute the food are seminarians. Instead of hearing shouts and accusations of sneaking back for a second helping (as happened in A3), we have the full respect of being called "Father," and that does a lot to keep up our morale in our conditions of detention. As you can see, we have our privileges.*

*We do not have any contact with the Germans except in camouflaging the lights and receiving the packages. The most precious thing is that thanks to the church, we can have complete solitude for study, and after 9 PM for prayer—also from 6 AM until roll call at 8. I get up almost without difficulty, because since I have practically no physical exercise, I do not need much sleep.*

*Today we decided—Fyodor T. Pianov, Yuri Pavlovich Kazachkin, Yuri, and I—to have a little drink. This means that we did not drink our lunchtime wine and we are going to drink it together at 3:00 PM, after which we will show up at the fiesta—sports tournaments, accordion and all sorts of foolishness intended to show that detainees have their morale in good shape. The last time, for July 14, some Spaniards enacted a bullfight. The bull was two guys under a blanket and a magnificent bull's head made out of cardboard. Among the mass of detainees there are professional artists and musicians. I am going to the fiesta now and I'll describe for you what I see. My dear Tomik, I want you to get a realistic look at our life and picture for yourself how Sobaka is living and working.*

*I have just come back from the fiesta. There was nothing interesting apart from the boxing. On the other hand I was able to go to Camp C for the first time, because they opened the access to it. You can see private houses there and people at the windows, which we haven't seen for six months. Then we had a little drink, with each of us drinking up his half liter, which produced a sensible effect. It's now time for the evening soup, and then vespers. Our friends are fulfilling their obedience at the kliros—they have to take on the responsibility of cantors. At first, it was Yuri who took on that function, but then it came the turn of*

*Yu. P., and today it's F. T. I am getting accustomed to using the tuning fork, but often I hit it without result and give the pitch by ear.*

*I saw Pavlik in a dream a little after we arrived at Compiègne. He embraced me and fondled me as children his age no longer do. That warmed my heart, but then I became disturbed, because it was precisely that night that a lot of airplanes flew over us, one of which machine-gunned our block and the neighboring block. In our barracks only two bullets hit, in the corridor, but in the neighboring one a man was wounded in the head, who then died. The incident was completely at random, like the last bombardment. All of a sudden I imagined that perhaps my birds were in danger. Tomkin! We will be reunited soon. It's unthinkable that this detention will be endlessly prolonged!*

*Thanks to the good weather, we are going to spend more time outside. Describe for me the details of your life and little unimportant things about the children.*

*Christ be with you, my dearly beloved Tomkin, and with the children. Tell Ladik that this drawing is for her. I am waiting for our interview. We must not be in a hurry to say everything but must concentrate clearly on what is most important. As for the rest, we will express it in letters. Above all we must not consider this visit as a cruel moment of our separation but as the prelude to our reunion.*

*I embrace my Tomik with all my strength.*
*Sobaka.*

## 13
## August 16, [1943]

*Dear Tomik,*

*At daybreak I wanted to speak again with my Tomik. I open my eyes every day at 6:00 AM as if I had an alarm clock, but it happens that I give myself a little break until 7:00 AM. I get up with no trouble. You ask me if I smoke early in the morning but the question is a strange one seeing that I take communion every day of the week except two. It's time for roll call.*

*I embrace you with all my heart.*
*Sobaka.*

*P.S.: If possible, send me some silk paper for our notes and a red and blue pencil.*

## 14
## September 4, 1943

*Dear Tomik,*

*Keifer was sent off the day before yesterday. There are reasons to assume he will travel through Germany to a camp near Vienna.*[24] *They say it's a model camp. We are all shaken by this departure. He took the matter with courage and optimism, but he is sad to be further away from his wife. The reasons he was chosen and taken away from our group are totally obscure. It is disturbing to think that it might be because he submitted a request for his liberation, because he is not the only one to have done that. Along with him 1100 men left, and 1927 remain. His most pressing request is for someone to take care of his wife. I reassured him with the promise that you would not leave her. He is in a very elevated spiritual condition. He took communion the day he left. We celebrated a moleben for him. Many people came to give him a warm goodbye; he has made plenty of friends here, and also enjoys everybody's respect as head man of the barracks.*

*What about the visit? Don't despair if they don't let you come, because we will see one another again soon. I intend to be home for Christmas. Life rolls along without change apart from the fact that they give us a quarter of a round loaf of bread instead of a sixth as they did at first. Three hundred grams is more than enough and you must not send biscuits, which deprive someone else of rationing coupons. I dedicate a lot of time to the French language. Every day I give my course in Russian from 11:30 AM to noon and in return I get a French course from 4:00 to 5:00 PM.*

*I am worried about how you are eating because they say that the situation has gotten significantly worse in Paris. As for us, on the contrary, we eat better than we could do in Paris. I am waiting impatiently to know how you lived through the bombardment.*

*Dear Tomik, when are we going to live a normal life? How will I get acquainted with Pavkin again? Doubtless he will begin to talk soon.*

*Our church is dedicated to St. Nicholas. I have received the Greek book and I was able to celebrate in Greek. If you can, send me one or two books of prayers and inexpensive little crosses.*

*I embrace my birds ardently. Christ be with you.*

*I am getting up later because of the darkness. I have trouble getting up. Don't despair if they don't allow us the visit, because we will see one another one way*

24 George Kazachkin was taken to Buchenwald, then to Dora.

*or the other. What news is there about the apartment? Send me some Sterogil*[25] *if you find any so that I can do battle against the cold. One more time, I embrace you.*

*Sobaka.*

**15**
**September 12, 1943**

*My dear Tomik,*

*I'm just going to write you two words while I have the chance. My next letter runs the risk of being delayed for two weeks because the man who passes them along was taken away. There are some departures in the air. Doubtless we will escape the next one, given that we were not summoned to the prerequisite medical visit. All the same I am afraid that sooner or later this is inevitable. As for now, this must not frighten you because it will not be for long. If it happens, you must not get discouraged. Distance plays no role because God is with us everywhere.*

*Today we are celebrating the anniversary of my priesthood*[26] *and on this account they gave us some wine. Fr. Andrey celebrated a moleben and spoke warmly. I prayed for my birds.*

*Tomik, you must not let your soul weaken an iota. Mobilize all the Church's resources in order not only to guard yourself for our future joy and spiritually intensive life and work, but also to grow spiritually. Everything is going well, Tomik. In what concerns our material life, we are eating more than people who are free.*

*I embrace my cherished birds and bless them. Christ is with you and no one is against you. I embrace the wife of Yuri Pavlovich,*[27] *for whom I pray every day.*

*P.S.: Yuri is asking for money from his father, who is at Feuillardes,*[28] *and that people not take steps to have him liberated. Mother Maria is in Poland.*[29]

---

25  Tonic medicine.
26  Fr. Dimitri was ordained priest on September 12, 1937, in St. Alexander Nevsky Cathedral in Paris.
27  Kazachkin.
28  Property rented by Danilo Skobtsov in the Val d'Oise, where he cultivated the land and from where he provided vegetables to the prisoners.
29  Incorrect information, although Ravensbrück, which is located in Pomerania, is not far from Poland.

## 16
## September 1943

*Dear Tomik,*

*I don't know if there will be an opportunity to write you next week. Don't worry about the visit. It's the prologue to our definitive and speedy reunion. We will soon be reunited. Prepare an account of yourself for me, because everything that concerns me is known to you. One cannot imagine better conditions—daily services, studies, a life for the four of us in our own quarters. We have enough food. Recently they have been feeding us considerably better. From time to time there is soup from the Red Cross. Thanks to your packages we have supper every evening. I feel neither weakness nor fatigue as I used to on walks. There is hardly any difficulty in getting up in the morning. I rise at 6:00 AM, we go to bed a little earlier, and during the day I can take a nap. I don't suffer from the heat. Although the air is stifling in the barracks, in our quarters it is fresh. We open the window at night. The tensions with Fr. Dimitri have more or less settled down. Our spiritual life is getting back to normal. Apart from my New Testament studies I have gotten down to a collection of personal pre-communion prayers. When I finish it I will write you with more details.*

*When I have seen you I would like to be able to imagine your life with all its difficulties. I received your package yesterday. Thank you, my Tomik. Everybody particularly enjoyed the tobacco and the tuning fork. I am sure that the Lord will not leave my birds without a roof. Who knows—in October will the two of us be in the process of looking for an apartment? I would love to organize my life and my work on different foundations. I don't want to predict anything and I remain at the disposition of the Church, but I would prefer—for your sake and mine—to be less of a parish priest. What I mean is that I would like not to be the only one to do all the work. In spite of all my love for our parish of the Protection, I don't dread being discharged when I return. In the meantime I don't want to break relations with the choir so that I can continue to celebrate with them.*

*We're lighting the vigil lamp. I give you a big hug. Imagine our meeting more simply. I will soon come back home. Embrace everyone and especially Tanya and Sonia.*

*Dimsky.*

## 17
## September 18, 1943

*My dearly beloved Tomik,*

*So we have seen one another again. This visit was like an irruption into another life and I don't know whether it took place or not. I neither told you nor asked you the things that were essential. Doubtless it is impossible in conditions of that sort. After the visit we had a general meeting. They took away Afstafyev and transferred Gornstein, and then they brought him back after the intervention of Fr. Andrey.*

*I am still under the impact of our meeting. I think back about how my Tomik prepared herself and how you were moved. I am impatiently awaiting your letter in which you tell me your impression of this visit. For the first two days afterwards my captivity appeared more unbearable to me. I experienced in a more real way the absurdity of our separation, from the human perspective. But now I glimpse its positive side, because it interrupted the countdown of days since February, and now a new countdown has begun with the assurance that this one will be shorter. I was not able to grasp your spiritual condition. Your letters brought me more than that meeting. It is certainly due to the very circumstances of your visit which, at the moment it arrived, created a particular state of mind that obscured your fundamental state.*

*The next day I received your wonderful package. We feasted and prayed for you before the meal. The enormous packet of butter caused me some worry. Do my birds know that sort of wealth? For me the essential thing is that you are healthy and safe. I beg you to keep the major part of the gifts people give for yourselves. You should know that our food exceeds the norm of what people at liberty are eating. There are even days that we don't finish our bread ration, that is, if I am satisfied! The day you arrived, rumors were flying concerning two sudden departures, but then they stopped and life took up its normal course again. I am sitting in the sanctuary of our chapel at the big table where I study and which serves for the proskomedia.*

*I am waiting for my Russian class. The classes in Russian and French are given on alternate days.*

## 18
## September 19, 1943

*Vladyka's arrangements concerning Fr. Andrey have created a strange atmosphere for us. Up to this point we have formed a united spiritual family with a single work of service and grouped primarily around the person of Fr. Andrey, who enjoys general esteem and authority. Our community pays no attention to jurisdictional divisions. We share in the same trial and we taste the same consolation from the Church, in which the divine will has reunited priests from different jurisdictions. Why be in such a hurry to destroy our liturgical communion for the sake of rumors about the moral faults of a priest who is deprived of any opportunity of opening his mouth to defend himself? Even supposing there is a foundation to these accusations, why not judge the man when he gets out of prison, when he will be able to present himself before his judges? (Not to mention that he is being judged by authorities under whom he does not fall canonically.) Even the law of the Old Testament gave the accused more liberty: "Does our law judge a man before it hears him and knows what he is doing?" (John 7:51). This haste to punish Fr. Andrey is doubtless explained by the fact that he lacks the freedom to throw off the mud with which he is covered by individuals who are at liberty. But why get us prisoners mixed up in the matter? Why disturb our peace and create an obstacle to the work we are accomplishing? The only explanation is that to the persecution of the civil power it is necessary to add ecclesiastical persecution in order to demonstrate that the Church authorities have nothing in common with this criminal. Instead of moral support and consolation for a priest who has been submitted to harsh trials, they cast a stone at him.*

*Even if the accusations were justified, why not leave this man in peace as long as he is in prison? If he were free, if he occupied an important place and had constituted a stumbling block for the church community, it would be different. But here in captivity, who is interested in his canonical transgressions? Nobody here knows his past. We judge him on his present, and we love and respect him. It is all too easy to throw mud on a man who is gagged without worrying about the consequences! The way Fr. Andrey's accusers have conducted themselves reflects the level of their morality—they are cowardly toadies. But what harms us the most is that our well-loved hierarch has ordered us to follow the line of these "pastors." If it were possible for me to cease to love him, this incident would have had less impact on me, but my love for him does not allow me to remain silent.*

*After all this time I have ties of friendship with Fr. Andrey, I confess to him, and we celebrate almost every day at the same eucharistic table. We share our joys and sorrows. The stories he has told have acquainted me with his family and vice versa. United in spirit, we gather the tortured and unhappy people around the holy chalice.*

## 19
### September 20, 1943

*Dear Tomik,*

*To the best of my understanding, I have been prohibited from concelebrating with Fr. Andrey. Show the second page of this letter to the metropolitan, then. If it seems to him that I am making too much of this incident, explain to him that our liturgical unity constitutes the central moment in our little life here and that it is a grave thing to destroy that union. Besides, we do not wish to take part in any way in the hateful persecution against our companion in captivity and our brother in Christ. Even if we were to discover that these accusations were well-grounded—and in fact they are false—the vileness of these accusations would not be lessened in any way. The vileness consists in the fact that the persecution is ill-timed. You don't kick a man when he is down.*

*Be brave, my Tomik. Some wonderful day will come when this trial is behind us. We will be seasoned troops, more patient, more courageous. It seems to me that we used to be rather timid in our approach to life. Explain to Ladik that the icon I sent her is worn by many prisoners. The Catholic priests distributed them. I wore it under my cassock, and now it's Ladkin who will wear it so that she will think more often of Sobaka.*

*I bless you as well as the little ones. Christ be with you. I embrace Tomik and the birds tenderly.*

*Sobaka.*

### Letter to Metropolitan Eulogius
### September 18, 1943

*Your Eminence, Dear Vladyka:*

*Thank you very much for the cassock and for your good treatment of Tamara and me. They are a great comfort in our trial. I thank God for His great mercy towards us all. We heard with great joy of the meeting of the Sobor and the election of a patriarch. Will this event have any impact on our church life in exile? We heard that the Russian Church is inviting the exiled clergy and laity to unite with her, although any postponement of our decision awaiting a more auspicious time will lead to the Russian Church's refusal to receive us. This decision is dictated by the impossibility under future normal conditions of conducting the selection of clergy based on indications of a sincere, not opportunistic attitude toward the Russian church. It would be extremely interesting to me, Vladyka, to know your thoughts on this question.*

*What a shame that I cannot take the metro and come to see you! I thank you for coming, in spite of your poor health, to the parish feast of our church, the day of the Protection of the Mother of God. Glory to God, I hear that our parish affairs are going well and everyone is happy with Fr. Stephan.*[30]

*We have a little church community here. The day before yesterday we received a Russian Protestant into Orthodoxy. Fr. Andrey is the one who forms the core of the group because he enjoys the esteem of the Russians as well as the French. During the months we have lived together I have gotten to know him well. I value him greatly as a man who is truly worthy of confidence. We had a group of about twenty Greeks for whom we celebrated the liturgy in French and Greek. Fortunately they were set free. I try to dedicate my free time to the study of Holy Scripture. I hope to be able to finish a course on the Gospel within a month. My students are F. T. Pianov and Yuri Skobtsov. In this way the days pass quickly. Lately, though, our captivity weighs on us more than before because it has been seven months that we have been behind barbed wire.*

*Here, Vladyka, is the succinct description of our life. Our chapel is large enough to contain a hundred people. It was full only once, on July 14,*[31] *when we celebrated a liturgy in French. Otherwise the daily liturgies gather seven or eight people out of the twenty Russians who are present here.*

*Again I implore your prayers, dear Vladyka, and your blessing. May God give you strength and health.*

*Your loving*
*Priest Dimitri*

**20**

**October 1, 1943**

*My beloved Tomik,*

*I have once again entered into the rhythm of the camp, which was disturbed by our meeting. You must not judge my state of mind by what you saw during our meeting because I was not in my normal state. Even though I suffer*

30 Fr. Stephan Ieromin.
31 July 14 is Bastille Day, the French equivalent of Independence Day.

*constantly from our separation, I am not nervous or disturbed. Our life is measured. Even if it had to stretch out a long time in these conditions, there would be no reason to fear that it would be detrimental. The most important thing is partaking almost daily of the holy gifts, as well as my constant theological studies. As far as the little disagreeable things in life with four people are concerned, I am used to them.*

*All my concern is for you because your life is much harder. You imagine my life as the most painful trial. In reality, behind the barbed wire I am sheltered from all the troublesome and dangerous things that threaten you. Your primary duty is to stand firm. I pray fervently for my birds. There is no reason to be depressed, because more than half the trial is over. It is a question of months, and every passing day brings us closer together.*

*October 2. Concerning myself, I think I will leave the camp in better shape than I was in before, because the last few months before my arrest were beyond my strength. The atmosphere in which I worked was too tense. That's why when I leave here I will be a better support for you. I think I am less afraid of life than before.*

*The atmosphere in our quarters has calmed down. We have grown more accustomed to one another. Fr. Andrey moved to the next room. F. T. replaced him. The tensions come above all from the relations of conflict between Fr. Dimitri Sobolev and Fr. Andrey. In my last letter I forgot to tell you that our chapel—which they were threatening to take away from us—was saved thanks to Fr. Andrey.*

*Give me news of the Church. Has anyone been in contact with Seraphim Liade?*

*Last Sunday our choir gave a little concert. We sang (1) "It is truly right" in the hierarchical version; (2) "Give rest, O Lord, to the souls of Thy servants"; (3) "Holy God" and "Before Thy cross"; and (4) "The angel cried." The public seems to have appreciated it, and my tuning fork served me well. On Sundays I no longer celebrate morning liturgy because it is too dark. These days I celebrate every third Sunday and twice during the week.*

*October 3. Write me more details about your life so that I have a better picture of it. Start writing in advance, like a diary. Where we live the atmosphere is as good as ever. We joke and tell anecdotes. Some Russians stop by and see us. We read newspapers and trade rumors. We continue to study the New Testament, organize choir rehearsals, and train chanters.*

*I think constantly about my birds. I imagine how we will organize our lives so that my Tomik will be happier. I think living together without the heaviness of a community house would lighten our existence.*

*I have learned to do my own mending and I am using my skill on my cassock, which I am repairing with some pieces of the old one that is in tatters. I will try to send you the bottles and my old summer cassock. If you can get some rabbit-skin mittens, send me a pair. Sobaka has hands that freeze during roll call, especially early before liturgy. I will send you back the leather gloves, which are not warm enough.*

*Forgive me, Tomik, for weighing you down with requests. All this can wait and only if it does not require too much searching for you.*

*I give you a big hug, my tenderly loved Tomik. May Christ be with you and the children. Tell Ladkin that I think about her all the time and that I am praying for her. Be cheerful and joyful. Everything will be over soon and we will be together again.*

*Your Sobaka.*

## Letter from Tamara to Fr. Dimitri[32]
## October 1, 1943

*My dear, my "piossik"[33] whom I love so much,*

*I write you from Ju's[34] house, where I stay when I have to spend the night in Paris, because at our house[35] chaos rules and some wildlife is roaming about. She is glad to receive me. We have grown much closer. She is inconsolable and it is very hard to help her. All the same I confide my Christian experience to her and she is drawn by religion, which is already a lot. You will do well to pray for her. It's indispensable.*

*Yesterday I received your letter and Anatoly's dated the 24th. It's terribly quick! I am happy that you are all together and that everything is going well. I have also just received your note of September 12—that is, from before our meeting. I have just come from the dry cleaner's, where I picked up your black*

---

32 Among the letters received from Compiègne there was a letter from Tamara addressed to her husband. Perhaps she had made a copy of it or else she was not able to send it.

33 Diminutive of *pios*, "dog."

34 Judith Kazachkina.

35 This refers to the house on Lourmel which, after the arrest of the group of Orthodox Action, resembled, according to a witness, "a devastated beehive." The Gestapo made forays there. The parish alone continued to function.

*jacket, and I'm going to send it to you. Do you need your gray vest? Answer me by letter because I don't want to burden you too much. Send me back your torn cassocks so that I can mend them. The priest from Chaville did something that touched me—he brought me his cassock, which I can alter so that it fits you, because it is very wide and very long. Did you receive the ink and the thread in the package for Anatoly? Do you need underwear? What you have must be tattered. You didn't tell me whether the last package for the church arrived, with the candles and so forth.*

*I am completely occupied with the move. Tomorrow I have to transport the coal and do a lot of other things. I have to empty out your room before the tenth, because it has been rented. I have to gather everything in the large room, but I don't have anybody to help me and I am suffering from having to turn everything that was in your room upside down because it is so filled with you—your study was a sort of confessional.*

*Dimzik, my love, I am languishing much more since our meeting. It's as if they showed me to you the way people show a nice surprise from a distance and then brutally they tore away Tomkin's better half. It's inhuman. But don't fear, I won't let them beat me down. Inside, I am always the same. I accept this cross completely. It's just that my nerves have undergone that rough trial by waiting and that sword of Damocles. Are they leaving or will they stay? People say there is a slowdown in the transports. Provided that God helps us!*

*Tell me, in your letter, in what state Astafyev left. Did he receive communion? His mother is desperate. Did he have any money apart from the hundred francs you gave him? I feel awkward in regard to her and Ju because I still have my husband in France while they are condemned to not having any news for a long time from those they love.*

*I haven't been able to see Vladyka again because it's a very personal meeting. Dimik, I want you to know that Vladyka was not at all favorable to the idea of forbidding you anything, understanding that it was going to destroy your ecclesiastical life, which was already very well established—he wrote me this in two letters and said personally that he was going to leave things as they were. But then after reflecting or perhaps being influenced by someone, he wrote me that they could not let you ignore the prohibition and that since you had an antimension of your own you could accommodate yourself to it. You must not believe that he adopted a purely formal position. He was very disturbed by that story, and that was when he told me that he could not conceal the truth from you. I am going to give him your reply, but first I want to speak to Fr. Sergius*[36] *about*

36 Fr. Sergius Bulgakov.

*it because he understands you so well, and I already spoke to him about it after
our meeting. He said it would be bad timing for you to get into conflict with Vladyka and that you will certainly find the least painful solution to this problem.
It is regrettable that Fr. Andrey presented the story to his wife incorrectly, not
as something that concerned him personally but as a general jurisdictional matter, which is totally false.*

*Where you are right is that this question should not have been posed at this
time in the unusual circumstances in which you find yourselves. Vladyka understands, but as an administrator he must be careful that the canons are respected.
At bottom you should understand that he appreciates you and respects you as a
confessor, as I have already told you and written you. Fr. Sergius finds that to be
very important and significant for Vladyka himself. Do you understand, Dim?*

*How I suffer at being the bearer of this bad news, which poisoned that meet-
ing which was already so difficult!*

*All my renters have left. Zhenya and I are by ourselves with the children. We
live in a state of peaceful co-existence. From time to time Zhenya does not feel
well but these are not crises. She is most of all attached to Pavkin, who is already
capable of walking by himself for a long time while pushing his stroller in front of
him. He is astonishingly robust and strong and not at all nervous. Ladkin is very
affectionate with me. I want to enroll her in a little private school so that she can
meet other children, which is indispensable to her. Do you agree? The directress
made a good impression on me. Sonia's daughters have been to that school.*

*The day of the Exaltation of the Cross, at Vespers, Lialia Godseridze[37] passed
away. I received the news the day of her burial but I went right away to see them.
Kolia is crushed. Liulia is brave and is a support to her father. The prince is with
them. Poor child! I want to invite her to spend a little time with us.*

*I see Dik[38] fairly often. He is very nice and attentive with me. Tanya is stay-
ing in the countryside with Masik.*

*Saturday—I am waiting for the truck that is going to bring my coal and
my things. Ju greets you very cordially. She is inconsolable and it is very difficult to comfort her because she has no religious experience. Romochka[39] is over-
whelmed, too, but her faith sustains her. Sophia Veniaminovna came back from
staying with the nuns in very good shape, and she sends you a hug. It's Sophia*

37 A family friend of the Klepinins. Nikolai Godseridze was my godfather.
38 Dik is the nickname of Vladimir Pokrovsky, husband of Tatiana Klepinin, sister of
   Dimitri, whose son Andrey is nicknamed Masik.
39 Romane Kliachkina, a great friend of the family, was able to escape arrest thanks
   to the intervention and prayers of Fr. Dimitri.

*Alexeyevna who helped me pack. She's marvelous—so calm and brave—and I love her like a sister. The only thing is that I don't do anything for her and she does so much for me.*

*Dimzik, what good fortune we have to have so many good and true friends!*

*Pray on Tuesday for Lialia. This will be the ninth day and I am going to see them. We're going to celebrate a Panikhida.*

*May God watch over you, my little boy, my good Dimsky. How I would love it if Pavkin resembles you! Ladik sends you a big hug, she talks about you all the time so tenderly. I squeeze you in my arms, my little sobachik. Zhenya embraces you good and tight and asks you to pray for her and her sons. Gulia is in Berlin.*

*May Christ be with you. Thank you for your tenderness and your constant encouragement.*

*Your Tomkin, always brave.*

## 21
## The eve of my feast day (November 7, 1943)[40]

*My dearly beloved Tomik,*

*It has been a long time since you have had news of Sobaka. I received your letter, the package for the church, and the package of vestments. I will try to send the empty boxes back to you, but they don't leave us packing paper or string and they puncture the paper cups. In the future I will force myself to find paper and string.*

*How are you, my birds? I console myself knowing that you are warm. Today we, too, lit our stove. I don't know if there will be enough fuel, but in any case it won't be so damp.*

*Tomik, the fact that our captivity is prolonged weighs more on me, but I will not give in to discouragement. I try to study. Try to see Vladyka again in a few days, recopy my letter and give it to him. Listen to his response, try to obtain something precise, not vague words. What awaits us is to be excluded from the Russian Church if we don't decide, because as a whole the Church of the emigration is guilty toward the Russian Church because of the schemes of people like Anastasy,[41] Shakhovskoy,[42] and company. The moment is now or never to*

40 November 8 is the feast day of St. Dimitri on the Julian calendar (liturgical date October 26).
41 Bishop Anastasy Gribanovsky.
42 Fr. John Shakhovskoy, archimandrite from the jurisdiction of Metropolitan

distance ourselves from them. If Vladyka thinks that I have come under the influence of Fr. Andrey, set him straight, because Fr. Andrey has not exerted any pressure on me. For me the most important thing has been the tenor of the council of the Russian Church and the election of the patriarch, which remove all obstacles to our reunion. The Russian Church has been spiritually victorious over Bolshevism and we are assisting in the renaissance of faith in Russia. It depends on us to participate in this joy or to be pushed aside—perhaps forever. Ask Vladyka if he has any information about the Russian Church's judgment about us.

Good night, my birds, I will finish my letter tomorrow. I am going to pray for you (I am in the church). I will bless you with the altar cross and I will go lie down until they put out the lights at 10 o'clock. My dear Tomik, tomorrow is my feast day and I will be with you in prayer and with my friends, with whom doubtless you will be spending the day. It seems to me that Tanya is not happily married. That's what I sense. Try to be a support to her if that's the case. We're going to celebrate a Moleben to Saints Anthony and Theodosius.

Try to see Vladyka before the next courier and don't leave him until you have a precise reply. If nothing changes I intend to ask him for my canonical release, but don't tell him that for the moment. We have to save our ecclesiastical organization, because if we keep the status quo, stone will not remain upon stone after the war.

Tomik, F. T. asks his wife to send him his mittens. We are good friends, he and I, and he has a heart of gold. I am waiting for the package sent by my Tomik for my nameday tomorrow or the next day. I am upset to bother you about the ink, but the blue ink you sent me runs on all the nice paper I have. It's useless to send it because they confiscate it from us. Send the black Waterman. It's important for my notes on the New Testament.

I am preparing myself psychologically to spend the winter here and let go of my dreams of being liberated before spring. Tomik, time passes quickly if we are strong morally. We will be, with God's help.

Tomik, here are the passages I have prepared for you to read: James 1:2–5; 2:20–21; Romans 8:18; 1 Corinthians 10:13; 2 Corinthians 1:3–5, 4:17, and 8:1–2; Ephesians 6:8; Philippians 1:29; Colossians 4:2; 1 Thessalonians 5:16–19; 1 Timothy 6:12; 2 Timothy 2:3–7; 3:12; Hebrews 2:4–12 and 13:2–14.

From the Psalms, I have chosen 18, 22, 26, 28, 30, 31, 33, 38, 41, 44, 45, 56, 61,

Eulogius, celebrated in Germany. He would later become archbishop of the Orthodox Church in America. At the moment of the invasion of the USSR by Germany in 1941, he had published a text in which he expressed the hope that Hitler would put an end to the communist regime.

*62, 64, 65, 68, 70, 83, 90, 95, 120, 138, 146, and 148. I recite them as a morning rule of prayer, primarily during roll call.*

*I try to imagine your life, the children romping around the house, and you and Zhenya occupied with the household. I am very happy that the atmosphere is not as tense as in Paris. Chase all the gloomy thoughts away with the Jesus Prayer. Take communion as often as possible. Think about life in the future in the service of the Church, an energetic and active life. The trial we are experiencing now will pass like a bad dream.*

*I have a new pastime—chess. It's a remarkable way of escaping reality. Tomkin!—I feel my little puppies very near. Write me if Keifer's wife is sending him any packages and whether she is corresponding regularly with him. I am waiting impatiently for your Tuesday letter. Embrace Tanya, Zhenya, and all our friends.*

*Ladik, my dear one, I am waiting for a letter from you, so hurry up and learn to write! I hope with all my strength to see you again and I pray fervently for you. I thank you for praying for me with Tomkin. It is certainly your prayer that helps me in this camp. On this paper I cannot draw anything properly. May God watch over you, my dear birds.*

*Your Sobaka.*

*P.S.: Here is the house where I live (drawing). Our window is in the middle. Send me a photo. I'd love to know what Pavkin looks like now.*

## 22
## November 20, 1943

*My dear little Tomik,*

*We have set up our new chapel, because they took away the old one to house people. The new one is in a separate barracks, on the parade grounds where the Catholics celebrate. A partition separates it from the rest of the barracks. This church reminds one of that of Clamart*[43] *but larger, with wood of a lighter color. Tomorrow morning (Sunday) we will celebrate there for the first time. From the street, if you stand close to the monument, you can easily hear the chanting through the open doors. I didn't receive my package from the feast until the thirteenth. Unfortunately the rabbit paté was spoiled. As far as the food was concerned, we rinsed it in vinegar and ate it hungrily. It works better not to send perishable products. Thanks to Zhenya for the chocolate, but she should keep it*

43 The church of Ss. Constantine and Helen in the Parisian suburb of Clamart.

*for her children instead. They need it more. I am worried about the decree con-cerning the Latvian nationals. What are you going to do?*[44] *Try to wait until the last minute. Wouldn't it be possible for you all to become Russian refugees?*

*Today we had to remain for an hour and a half exposed to the cold. I had enough clothing but my feet were cold in spite of two pairs of wool socks. Our only recourse was to dance in place. In our quarters we make a fire once a day when we prepare supper. During the day we freeze, and I spend most of the time in bed with my feet wrapped up. I go to bed for real at 9:00 PM and they put out the lights at 10:00 PM. I study lying down. Right now I am in bed. It is a blessed time.*

*I am waiting impatiently for your letter and in particular for news about Church affairs. If Vladyka responded before that he didn't have any information about the situation in the Church, I entreat you to go back and see him again, because he must have information by now. I see clearly that we must cease to be a Church of the emigration. We must not be excluded from an important eccle-siastical process but rather we must find ourselves back in touch. It is an essen-tial problem. We are at risk of remaining cut off from all participation in the life of the Church. I think the Church of the emigration deserved a punishment of this sort. Don't speak to anybody about my intention of asking for a canoni-cal release.*

*My dearly beloved Tomik, you're not depressed, are you? Soon everything will be behind us and there will be lots of big and interesting things ahead of us. (Burn my letters.)*

*Good night, my tenderly loved Tomik. May Christ be with you and with the little ones. Embrace Zhenya, Tanya, and all of our loved ones. I strongly advise you to read* Christ's Witnesses *by Marc Escholier. Till tomorrow.*

**Sunday.** *We celebrated in the new church, which is much better than the previ-ous one. Instead of beds turned on end, we have an iconostasis made with light-colored panels, the color of the walls. We can take shelter in there and our feet aren't as cold because it has a wooden floor.*

*We need charcoal for the church, and Yuri is asking for his blue stikharion.*[45] *He'll send back the one he has so it can be mended.*

*Thank you, Tomik, for the icon. It is the most beautiful I have ever had. It is hanging above my bed, and when I serve I put it on the altar. There, Tomik—*

---

44 Tamara, an émigré from Riga, had a Latvian passport. This decree obliged her to check in with the commissariat.

45 Liturgical vestment.

*that's our news. All the same, there is preparation for a departure. Every time the hope increases of staying but it is anguishing nevertheless. As God grants.*

*May God watch over you as well as my birds. I embrace you tenderly along with Zhenya, Tanya, and all our friends. Send me a photo of you. I have some rheumatism in my shoulder as I did at the time of Jouvenet.*[46] *It's bearable. Ahead of us there are only things to cause joy—springtime and so forth. In the wintertime we do well enough to get by one way or another. We're going to have a nice cup of tea and I'll return to my studies in bed.*

*Good night, my little Tomik.*

*Sobaka.*

## 23
## December 13, 1943[47]

*My tenderly loved Tomik,*

*Today, they unexpectedly assigned us to be transported, apparently to Germany. This departure also includes Yuri, Fr. Andrey, Anatoly, Klubov, Zhdanovsky, Makarov, Skolozubov, Onikei, Diakonov, Tkachenko, Mezintsev, and Gavrilov.*

*I am fully aware that the will of God is being carried out and that for me a new obedience in the Church is beginning. Fr. Dimitri remains behind. They have sent him his antimension and other things. I feel sorry for Fyodor Timofeyevich, who is desolate at our leaving. But how is my Tomik going to accept this new trial?—that is the only thing that causes me suffering. I am sure that the spiritual distance will not increase; borders do not matter. Everything will come to an end soon and we will be together again. In Germany I will be in greater security. Here some difficulties are shaping up and they are beginning to look at us suspiciously. When we are there we will lose ourselves in the mass of unknown people.*

*Promise me, my Tomik, to gather all your spiritual strength to remain in peace and in prayerful certainty that God will watch over us. Partake often of the holy gifts. Always stay among people who can support you. Don't let despondency or irritation take root in you, and run quickly and confess to a priest.*

---

46 After they were married, the Klepinins lived on rue Jouvenet, in the Sixteenth Arrondissement of Paris.

47 This was the last letter Tamara received. Much later a letter came to her from Buchenwald, written in German in a trembling handwriting and including his last blessing.

*Stay in contact with Fr. Sergius. Preserve your peace so that the children can get through this difficult period without a depression that could mark them for life.*

*And do it for me, too, so that when I return we can take up a joyful and active life. I will come back with a greater experience of life and doubtless with new spiritual strength, but worn out from the trial, and I will need your support even more. I'm sure everything will go fine. Console me with your bravery. That is the gauge of my well-being, because I am ready for everything except your suffering and your sadness.*

*I hope we will reestablish contact quickly and that they'll let us write letters.*

*Give a big hug to Tanya, Zhenya, Father Sergius, Sophia Veniaminovna, Kotya,*[48] *and all our friends, including Alyosha B.*

*My dearly beloved Tomik, Ladik, Pavlik, I clasp you in my arms and bless you. Every evening when I go to bed, I embrace the icon you sent me, I caress your photos as if they were you. I feel your presence so strongly, your love, your solicitude. Christ is with us, and all the rest is insignificant in comparison with His love for us.*

*Rejoice, my birds, we will see one another again soon.*

*Your brave Dimsky.*

---

48 Kotya is the nickname of Konstantin Mochulsky, man of letters and a great friend of the Klepinins.

# Recommended Reading

**Royal Monastic: Princess Ileana of Romania**
The Story of Mother Alexandra
*by Bev. Cooke*
*ISBN: 978-1-888212-32-7*
*$15.95*

*Through a life of selfless sacrifice, rock-hard faith, danger, and exile, Princess Ileana won her people's heart so thoroughly she is still revered by Romanians today.*

The life of a princess isn't all fun-filled travel, magnificent banquets, handsome princes, and beautiful clothes. It's also devotion to duty, sacrifice for your people, and a lot of just plain hard work. And if your country happens to suffer two world wars and a communist takeover in your lifetime, it means danger and suffering, exile and heartache as well.

Princess Ileana of Romania endured all this and more. But her deeply rooted Orthodox faith saw her through it all, and eventually led her in her later years to the peaceful repose of monasticism. But that life included sacrifice and hard work as well, because as Mother Alexandra she was called to build the first English-language Orthodox women's monastery in the United States—the Monastery of the Transfiguration in Ellwood City, Pennsylvania.

Princess Ileana's story is a thrilling tale of love and loss, danger and rescue, sacrifice and reward. Her inspiring life stands as a beacon of faith and holiness for young women of all times and nations to follow.

**Lynette's Hope:**
The Witness of Lynette Katherine Hoppe's Life and Death
*Edited by Fr. Luke A. Veronis*
*ISBN: 978-1-888212-99-0*
*$17.95*

*"Now we have to live whatever we have ever preached to others," Lynette Hoppe wrote in her journal. "I have been classified as having Stage 4 cancer (of four stages), and my prospects are rather grim. Nonetheless, I remain cheerful and hopeful and want to spend what years God grants me in joy and thanksgiving, serving as and wherever I can."*

With these sober yet hopeful words, Orthodox missionary to Albania Lynette Hoppe began the last journey of her fruitful life. In frank and poignant prose, Lynette's journals, newsletters, and website chronicled her struggles in the "valley of the shadow" as she faced impending death. Close family friend and fellow missionary Fr. Luke Veronis briefly tells the story of Lynette's life, then lets her writing speak for itself, showing how Lynette's radical faith and love for Christ transformed the tragedy of a young mother's untimely death into a powerful witness to the love and saving power of her Lord. Those who witnessed Lynette's passing agree that hers was truly a "beautiful death."

*These and many other inspiring books are available from Conciliar Press Ministries at www.conciliarpress.com.*